ARIZONA
Curiosities

Help Us Keep This Guide Up to Date

Every effort has been made by the author and editors to make this guide as accurate and useful as possible. However, many things can change after a guide is published—establishments close, phone numbers change, hiking trails are rerouted, facilities come under new management, etc.

We would love to hear from you concerning your experiences with this guide and how you feel it could be improved and kept up to date. While we may not be able to respond to all comments and suggestions, we'll take them to heart and we'll also make certain to share them with the author. Please send your comments and suggestions to the following address:

The Globe Pequot Press
Reader Response/Editorial Department
P.O. Box 480
Guilford, CT 06437

Or you may e-mail us at:

editorial@GlobePequot.com

Thanks for your input, and happy travels!

Curiosities Series

ARIZONA
Curiosities

QUIRKY CHARACTERS, ROADSIDE ODDITIES, &
OTHER OFFBEAT STUFF

Sam Lowe

The Globe Pequot Press

GUILFORD, CONNECTICUT

The prices and rates listed in this guidebook were con-
firmed at press time. We recommend, however, that you
call establishments to obtain current information before
traveling.

Cover photos: Sam Lowe
Cover design: Nancy Freeborn
Text design: Bill Brown
Layout: Deborah Nicolais
Maps created by XNR Productions, Inc. © The Globe Pequot Press
Photo on p. 281 courtesy of Scottsdale Community College. All
other interior photos by the author.

ISBN 0-7627-2547-8

Manufactured in the United States of America
First Edition/First Printing

To Lyn, my wife, who packed lunches, made sure I had enough clean underwear on overnight trips, and listened to my graphic and endless descriptions of petrified dinosaurs and 8-foot quails.

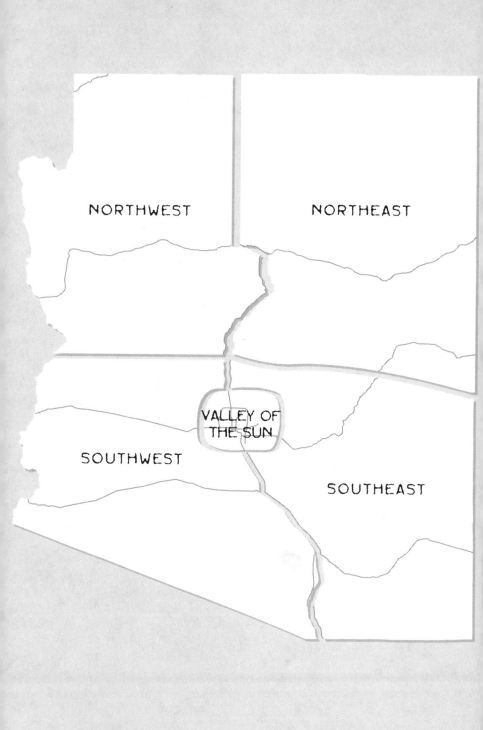

Contents

ACKNOWLEDGMENTS

A lot of kind and gentle folks helped me along the way. Marshall Trimble, the state's official historian, not only recommended me for the assignment but also was an invaluable resource when I needed background information.

Special thanks to Janice Griffith for showing me which Winslow corner to stand on; Sheldon Miller for arranging an interview with Zubaz, the big blue alien; David Schwarz, who found the 8-foot quail; Landon Osborn, who showed the way to the state's largest egg; Dewanne Hopson, who guided me across a snake bridge; Hoyt Johnson, who pointed out the world's only teal-arched McDonald's; and Bert Ijams and Susan Schepman for locating a downed spaceship.

To Archy McDonald, who knew the way to Skull Rock; Jennie Inman for directions to the Chloride Mural; Judy and Ron Spencer for details on staying aloft for forty-seven days; Helen Neuharth, who set up a meeting with a cotton-boll painter; Julie Brooks, who knows about sand fishing along the Hassayampa River; and Paul Wolterbeek, an expert on boojum trees.

Thanks to the people at the visitor centers, especially those in Kingman, Mayer, Flagstaff, Tucson, Willcox, Holbrook, Springerville, Show Low, Bisbee, Benson, Wickenburg, Patagonia, Yuma, Parker, and Lake Havasu City.

To Kathy Curley, who never doubted that I'd hear the voices at Window Rock; Althea Long and Joyce Eisert for an introduction to Arty Artichoke; Terri Noll because she knows Spawn personally; Bob Ware for sharing information about Baitman; Janie Magruder and Barbara Yost, wonderful writers who gladly shared information; Stan Brown for knowing where Leo the Lion crashed; and Jacki Mieler, who took me to Nothing for nothing. To Mary Norris and Josh Rosenberg, who guided me through the editing process.

And thanks to all the librarians and innkeepers, septuagenarians and historians, waitresses and peace officers, park guards and, yes, an occasional bartender, who took the time to help me out and never once asked for money or sent me on a wild goose chase.

INTRODUCTION

One day in August 2002 while driving north on Interstate 17 near Camp Verde, I passed an old Volkswagen bus, one of those trusty vehicles elevated to immortality by the Hippie Generation. It had flowers on the door panels, peace symbols on the rear windows, and a bumper sticker that read, "If you owned one of these, you'd be home now."

It was a reminder that Arizona is still in a state of populational transition. Most people who live here weren't born here. We came here because we didn't like the way things were back home. And once we established ourselves as official Arizonans by making that all-important phone call to relatives in the Dakotas and Minnesota to brag about mowing the lawn in November, we lobbied for new laws banning future immigration into the state.

Then we set about planting elm trees like the ones that used to line Main Street back home to give us some shade so the sun wouldn't frazzle our brains and turn us into zombielike creatures whose response to every weather forecast is, "Yes, but it's a dry heat."

But we come to love it here. The weather's nice a lot of the time, and in the winter we can snow ski in the morning and water ski in the afternoon, if we own a car that can travel 200 miles in under three hours.

And being from somewhere else is a good thing because we brought some pretty good idiosyncrasies along with us, and that's what this book is all about. With that in mind I set out on a 10,000-mile journey across my adopted homeland to see what's out there besides the Grand Canyon, the state's quintessential

Tour guides in Canyon de Chelly on the Navajo Reservation haven't given this face-in-a-rock an official name, but there's common agreement among both guides and tourists that it bears a striking resemblance to either a famous comedian or a former president.

icon that a substantial number of Arizonans have never seen. If my non-scientific survey is worth considering, more Japanese and Germans than Arizonans have inspected the Canyon. Most in-state residents, however, plan to go look at it. Some day. As soon as all those foreigners clear out so there's enough parking spaces for the locals.

The odyssey took me into deserts, libraries, mountain ranges, museums, visitor and historical centers, and yes, even an occasional saloon, but of course only when all else failed. I visited them in such places as Winslow, Chloride, Dolan Springs, Ajo, Patagonia, Yucca, Kayenta, and Dos Cabezas. I entered into serious discussions with a man who makes rattlesnake jerky, a woman who runs a bookstore on a cattle ranch, a woman whose husband bought her a 40-foot golf ball for her birthday, and a guy who crafts dinosaurs out of wrecked cars.

CROAKINGLY OFFICIAL

*A*rizona covers 114,000 square miles. It is the sixth-largest state in the union, and the only state of its size to have an official state amphibian that is less than 2 inches long. The Arizona tree frog was selected for that high honor in 1986, when elementary school children voted for it in order to promote environmental awareness.

Despite the prestige that goes along with the job, the green, gold, and sometimes bronze tree frog apparently does not relish its celebrity status, because it is rarely seen. It's not only small but also nocturnal, it lives only at elevations of 5,000 feet or higher, and it hibernates under rocks and logs most of the year, emerging only from May through September to procreate the species and look for official frog food.

The reason for this shyness becomes apparent with the revelation that Arizona's official state amphibian is a primary foodstuff for such critters as tiger salamanders, raccoon, snakes, and large insects, none of which has any respect for lofty status.

An old wrangler shoved his ten-gallon hat down firmly across his ears and explained the proper way to play cowboy golf. "They ain't nothin' to this game," he said. "You just swang and cuss and hope you can find your ball afterwards." Six patrons of a small-town watering hole offered to lead an after-dark expedition into the surrounding mountains where each swore he'd seen a flying saucer. They made the offer around 2:00 P.M. At the rate they were consuming UFO repellent, none of them was going to be standing when the sun went down.

An elderly man took me through the Jurassic Park he has created out of broken floor tiles and cement slabs and became very upset when I had to leave after three hours because, in his words, "you ain't even seen my good stuff yet." A woman in a museum proudly displayed a handkerchief that had been to two official functions in Washington, D.C., during the time of Abe Lincoln.

While zooming south on Interstate 19 between Tucson and Nogales, I keenly observed that the freeway signs listed the distances but not the speed limit in kilometers instead of miles. It's the only freeway in the United States with metric signs, mainly because the road is near the border with Mexico, where kilometers are the norm. But why metric for only distance? The speed limit along that stretch is 75 miles per hour, a speed most freeway drivers observe only when changing a flat tire. So if the speed limit were converted into kilometers per hour, it'd be 120 kph, which would be immediately translated into an excuse to drive 130 miles per hour.

My modus operandi was simple: Go to a town, stop at a town hall, police station, chamber of commerce, and yes, occasionally, even a saloon, and ask the basic question, "You got any weird things here?" The near-unanimous response was, "You're looking at 'em." But when pinned down for details, they usually admitted they were normal. Except for the woman who said she once wore the same dress every day for a month without telling her husband about it, just to see if he'd notice.

I found the people of my state to be friendly and hospitable, for the most part. A couple of times my inquiry was met with a certain aloofness and a rather curt response to the effect of, "Well, we most certainly don't have anything like that in our town." After further questioning, however, they relaxed and sent me out along dirt roads and pastureland trails, looking for such curiosities as a house built in the shape of an eagle (it was there, but so was a barbed-wire fence and a very large dog with slather on his lips and dismemberment on his mind, so I elected to save that one for Volume II).

I ate Indian fry bread at a roadside stand, stood in four states at the same time without ripping my blue jeans, laid flat on my belly to peer 900 feet straight down a canyon wall, and drove across a road that should have been banned by the Committee on Cruel and Inhumane Treatment of Motorized Vehicles.

It was a good time. In fact it was probably the most fun I've ever had with all my clothes on.

I'd do it all over again.

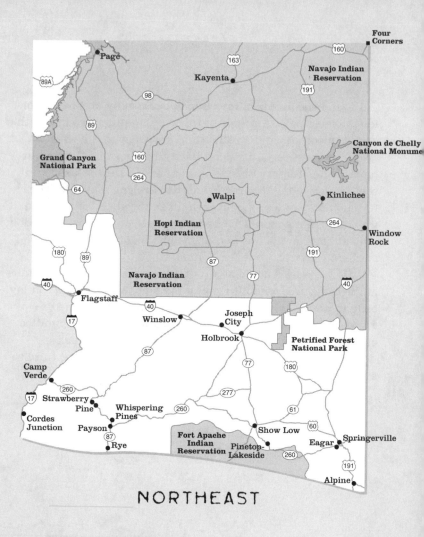

Four
Corners

{160}

Navajo Indian
Reservation

{163}

{191}

Kayenta

Page

{98}

{89A}

{89}

Canyon de Chelly
National Monume

Grand Canyon
National Park

{160}

{264}

{64}

Walpi

Kinlichee

Hopi Indian
Reservation

{264}

Window
Rock

{180} {89}

{191}

{40}

{87}

{77}

{40}

Navajo Indian
Reservation

Flagstaff

{17}

{40}

Winslow

Joseph
City

Holbrook

Petrified Forest
National Park

{77}

Camp
Verde

{180}

{260}

{277}

{17}

Strawberry

Pine

Whispering
Pines

{260}

{61}

{60}

Cordes
Junction

Payson

{87}

Rye

Fort Apache
Indian
Reservation

Pinetop-
Lakeside

Show Low

Eagar

Springerville

{260}

{191}

Alpine

NORTHEAST

NORTHEAST

Hi Yo Wormie
Alpine

I t's not quite Olympic-Games caliber, but the worm races are one of the major summer events in this White Mountain community. They're run on the second Saturday of July and are preceded by a short (naturally) worm parade.

The races are held in a tent behind Ye Olde Tavern on a 4-foot-square piece of plywood painted with rings. It's not head-to-head competition, however. Each worm is placed in the center ring and given two minutes to crawl, and the action can get furious. One worm, for example, raced right off the end of the racetrack to set a record that still stands. The winner is determined by distance, not speed.

Worm breeders can urge their steeds on by misting them with water from a spray bottle or by yelling words of encouragement like, "Win or you'll be sleeping with the fishes!" Entry fees are $5.00 per worm. Some of the money is returned as prizes, and the rest goes to charity.

According to local legend the first races also featured the coronation of The Robin, a person who was designated to eat all the losing worms between shots of tequila. The practice has been discontinued, allegedly because it gave the tequila a bad taste.

Worm fans and handicappers interested in more information may call (928) 339–4330.

THE CALL OF THE KOKOPELLI
Camp Verde

The kokopelli—or flute player—is a fertility symbol among the Hopi Indians, but the image doesn't always have cultural significance. For example, there's a huge kokopelli here that stands perpetual watch over such treasures as plaster Tweety Birds, plastic snakes, and a replica of the *Venus de Milo*. It performs this function at the Montezuma Trading Post, a tourist-oriented establishment that offers for sale, among other things, bumper stickers saying, "Lottery: A tax on people who are bad at math" and "Happiness is an empty holding tank."

Despite that wealth of merchandise, the kokopelli is probably the main reason most people stop. This is understandable. The sculpture stands 32 feet tall, is painted bright yellow, and is perched on a 6-foot base, so it dominates the skyline.

Lowell Johnson, one of the storeowners, says it's the world largest kokopelli and adds that nobody has challenged the claim. The sculpture is made of welded steel, cost $25,000, and weighs five and a half tons. It was created by Gerry Berg Sr. and his son, Gerry, who spent about forty-five days working on the project.

Flute players and others can see the giant musician just off Interstate 17 at Camp Verde.

The world's largest kokopelli plays its flute for tourists and bargain hunters at Camp Verde.

Montezuma's Castle suffers from a bad case of mistaken identity.

THE FULL MONTEZUMA
Camp Verde

The history of Montezuma Castle is well documented, considering that nobody wrote anything down when it was an active community. Through decades of research, archaeologists have established that Sinaguan farmers began building the 5-story, 20-room dwelling early in the 12th century and that it was abandoned about 300 years later.

They have also found that the name is a mistake. The famous Aztec chief Montezuma never spent a night here. Early white explorers thought Aztec refugees who fled Mexico during the Spanish conquest built it, but scholars have determined that neither Montezuma nor any of his followers made it this far north. Despite that, the misnomer remains the same, with some bureaucratic adjustments. Now it's Montezuma Castle National Monument.

The structure is well preserved on its original site in a cliff recess 100 feet above a valley, so visitors can look but can't touch. Unable to see it close-up and check the walls for plumb, those who come here are forced to speculate such imponderables as, "How'd they do that without Black and Decker and Home Depot?"

Those who wish to make similar observations and inquiries should take exit 289 off Interstate 17 at Camp Verde. For details, call (928) 567–3322.

DO THEY SERVE CHILI CORN CORNE?
Camp Verde

The annual Corn Fest, which cornvenes here every summer to honor the community's agricultural heritage, offers a variety of events for those corncerned about the status of corn. Among them are corn bobbing, corn shucking, corn baking, hog calling, and corn eating.

The corn-eating corntest got cornfusing, so they had to change the rules. In the beginning, corntestants were judged on how many ears of corn they could eat in two minutes. But they were eating too much, so the winner's now whoever eats the most in ten seconds without getting cornstipated.

Also on the agenda is the corny-story corntest. This event allows normal people to tell jokes like, "Question: Who was the most famous of all the Chinese philosophers? Answer: Cornfucius." And "Question: Why is cooked corn always placed in a corntainer? Answer: So it doesn't get corntaminated."

Winners in all events receive ceramic corn trophies and corngratulations. Losers get only corndolences. For full details cornsider calling (928) 567–0535.

THE LEGEND OF SPIDER ROCK
Canyon de Chelly National Monument

Several spires rise from Canyon de Chelly but two of them stand side by side and are much more noticeable than the others. The tallest is Spider Rock. The red sandstone monolith stands 800 feet above the canyon floor and is topped by some white rock. Its mate is Speaking Rock, which rises about 650 feet. They are awesome. So are the legends that surround them.

According to the Navajo creation story, Spider Rock takes its name from Spider Woman, a Navajo deity also cast in the role of disciplinarian for Navajo children. Legend says that after Spider Woman chose the top of Spider Rock as her home, parents told their children that the sun-bleached white rock at the top was actually the bones of little ones who didn't behave.

The other spire is called Speaking Rock, a lesser figure who serves as a snitch. When children are bad, the story says, the rock relates their misdeeds to Spider Woman, who swoops down from the top of her rock and eats them, then deposits their bones on the top of Spider Rock.

Both are readily visible from the South Rim drive at the canyon. Those who want a closer look from the canyon floor have to make arrangements with local guide outfits.

A WORK IN (SLOW) PROGRESS
Cordes Junction

At Arcosanti, a city-of-the-future prototype, "speed" is almost a four-letter word. The project has been under construction since 1970. It's not finished. It may not be finished in this generation. The man who dreamed it up may never see it completed.

That is not a problem for Paolo Soleri, the Italian-born architect/philosopher/artist who designed the city. His vision combines architecture with ecology to create "arcology," hence the name. If it ever is completed, it'll be home to about 7,000 people living and working in a close-knit environment. His philosophy defies conventional build-it-in-a-hurry and get-folks-in-it practices by extending the building deadline to whenever it gets done.

*Arcosanti may set a modern-day record for construction
longevity. The futuristic city has been in the building stages
for more than thirty years, and it's still not finished.*

There'll never be cars within the city, solar power will be
king, curved architecture is the standard, and density is a good
thing. The concept is pedestrian friendly, so the roads end outside the complex and pathways and benches take over. Solar
energy heats the buildings, and evaporative cooling fights off
the desert heat. Most of the buildings are half-spheres facing
south to take advantage of the winter sun. And the inhabitants
will live and work closely together to avoid sprawl.

Although the pace is slow, construction goes on. The music
center has been completed, and more housing/office space
should be done whenever it gets done.

Those interested in what the future may look like can tour
Arcosanti by taking the Cordes Junction exit off Interstate 17,
then following the signs. Tours are offered on the hour from
10:00 A.M. to 4:00 P.M. daily. For details call (928) 632–7135.

THE CASE OF
THE
BARE BEAR

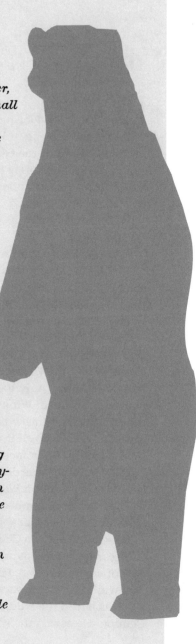

*I*saadore Christopher, a French settler,
has several claims to infamy. A small
community bears his name; so does a
nearby mountain. He also came home
once and found a bear in his grave.

In July 1882 Christopher killed a
large bear, skinned it, and hung the
carcass in his cabin. The next day
while he was gone, an Apache raiding
party attacked and burned the
cabin. A troop of U.S. soldiers in
close pursuit of the raiders arrived
on the scene while the cabin was
still engulfed in flames.

After extinguishing the blaze,
the soldiers discovered the remains
of the bear. Mistakenly assuming
that the carcass belonged to
Christopher, they dug a shallow
grave in a cornfield, held a solemn
burial service, and spoke kind words
about what a good man he had been.

Christopher returned the following
day, still very much alive. After survey-
ing the damage he built another cabin
that is still in use today. But after the
death of his wife in 1906, he moved to
California and was never heard from
again. The bear that stood (or laid) in
for him reappeared, in a sense, after
several years, when one of the cabin's
later occupants dug up the bones while
digging in a garden.

NOT EVERYBODY LIKED IKE
Eagar

Ever get to wondering what ever happened to Ike Clanton?

He earned a niche in Western lore as one of the participants in the gunfight at the OK Corral. According to historians he exited the scene shortly after the shooting began, so he lived to tell about it. But then he just sort of rode off into the sunset of history. Where'd he go?

Well, he died anyway.

Gunshot.

Had it coming, though.

The details are all in the Little House Museum, a four-building complex sitting on a ranch west of Eagar. Its roots trace from the days when cattle rustling was a way of life and murder was as common as chicken pox.

One building dates from 1885; others were added over the years. Today they're all part of the X Diamond Ranch, owned and operated by Winkie Crigler, who was born on the ranch and moved away only to attend college. Her grandfather started the spread; Winkie and her husband ran it until his death in 1985. That's when she decided the area needed a museum even though it was way out in the country.

The facility deals mostly with the history of Apache County, but one building was designed to house a carriage given to the couple by actor John Wayne, whose ranch adjoined theirs. Also on display are old musical instruments, newspaper clippings, clothing, and photographs.

So what about Ike Clanton?

According to one newspaper article, his career came to an abrupt end on June 1, 1887, when a lawman shot and killed him while serving a warrant. The reporter philosophized thusly:

"This ended the wild career of poor deluded, misguided Ike Clanton. He sowed the winds and harvested the whirlwind and his harvest is gathered into a narrow house six feet by two, and the panther, wolf and bear growl a fitting requiem over his grave..."

For details and directions, call (928) 333-2286.

FOR LOVE OF THE DOVE
Flagstaff

The Chapel of the Holy Dove is a little stopping-off place about 18 miles north of Flagstaff on Highway 180, a major route to the Grand Canyon. Passersby stop there to meditate and sometimes to get married, even though the structure holds about only ten people. First built in 1963 by Dr. Watson Lacy as a memorial to his brother, the little church was destroyed by fire in 1999, and there were no plans to rebuild it.

Then along came Christin McCracken of Flagstaff, who had dreamed since childhood of one day marrying her true love in the chapel. After learning of the fire, the teenager set out to restore the church so she'd have a place to get married in. She enlisted the aid of her father, a contractor, and several others and worked diligently for two years to complete the project.

Now, the chapel is better than ever and open to all who stop. The visitors pray and commune and often write prayers and messages on walls and ceilings. One asks that a prisoner be paroled, another asks that angels accompany a serviceman, and one says, "God Rocks!"

And Christin found the man of her dreams. He was one of the volunteers working at the chapel. They're not married yet, but when they do exchange vows, it'll be in the Chapel of the Holy Dove. "Or else," Christin said, "he's got to find someone else to marry."

A CHRISTMAS STORY
Flagstaff

Bob and Sally Trotter take Christmas seriously, even though it disrupts everything in their home from cooking breakfast to brushing their teeth. It's because they collect Nativity scenes, commonly called crèches.

They have more than 200 of them, and they put them on display every December. That means they have crèches in front of their house, crèches in the living room, crèches on the kitchen counters. Crèches in the bedrooms, crèches in the den. Crèches on the mantel over the fireplace, on the windowsills, on the staircase landings, and on every table in the house. They even have one in the bathroom.

"When I start unpacking every year, it looks like we're moving in," Sally Trotter said. Bob Trotter's mother, the late Virginia Y. Trotter, former Secretary of Education under Presidents Nixon and Ford, started the collection in the 1950s. She brought home crèches from more than sixty countries, and the current owners still add several every year.

The scenes are from such places as Switzerland, Uganda, Romania, Israel, Appalachia, and Argentina, and they're made of such materials as muslin, wood, porcelain, needlepoint, and corn husks. Sally Trotter said the tradition takes most of her time from late November through the Christmas season.

Occasionally the family puts some of the crèches on display at a local museum or allows school tours, but their home is not open to the public.

CAN WE TALK?

Flagstaff

Conversations with animals have been well explored in the fantasy worlds of television and movies, from *Dr. Doolittle* to *Babe,* from *Francis the Talking Mule* to *Mr. Ed.* But they're all make-believe. Dr. Con Slobodchikoff's effort to communicate with prairie dogs is real.

Slobodchikoff is a professor in the Biology Department at Northern Arizona University, teaching animal-behavior sciences. Through his research he has concluded that prairie dogs can, using a language of their own, talk with each other. And further, he says, humans can figure out what they're talking about if they just listen carefully.

Since the early 1990s the professor has recorded and analyzed prairie dog chitchat, particularly those dealing with the approach of potential predators. He has noticed the chips and bips are modified to describe different situations. For example, the sound they make for a hawk is different from the one used to signal the presence of a coyote. "They have one call for a person carrying a rifle," he said. "They view it as a threat and label it that. And they have a different call for a nonhunter."

But although he's been a friend of the prairie dogs for more than a decade, the creatures remain aloof toward Slobodchikoff. During our afternoon stroll through their village, every one of the little rascals scurried down their hole without so much as a howdy.

They probably recognize him, though. It's just that they have trouble pronouncing his name.

WALK BETWEEN THE BRANCHES
Flagstaff

The Museum Club was beset with a diminishing history for years after it opened in 1931. First it was billed as "the biggest log cabin in the world." Later it was downsized to "the biggest log cabin in the nation," and eventually to "the biggest log cabin in Arizona."

But through it all, one claim has remained unchallenged. The front entryway is still the largest doorway in the world made from a forked tree that was once struck by lightning. It's the remains of an old Ponderosa pine that was split by a lightning blast somewhere back around 1900. Two separate, but equal, branches emerged to form a giant Y. It was chopped down, hauled to the log cabin, and inverted across the building front so it looks like those who enter are walking between the knotty knees of a bowlegged cowboy.

The building underwent another fall toward oblivion in the 1970s after Interstate 40 displaced Route 66 through Flagstaff and cost the combination nightclub/museum much of its clientele. But in 1978 Martin Zanzucchi bought it, refurbished it, and brought it back to life as the Museum Club. Zanzucchi had to upgrade both interior and exterior, but one thing remains unchanged—patrons still have to walk between the branches of the old Ponderosa pine to get in.

The club is at 3404 East Route 66. For details, call (928) 526–9434.

SOMETHING FOR THE SLEEPLESS
Flagstaff

The annual Flagstaff Toys for Tots Bed Races USA has nothing to do with brushing, flossing, and getting into your jammies. Instead it's a sporting event that features up to fifty teams of bed-pushing athletes pitted against each other as they race through the streets of the city.

Each team is composed of five members—four pushers and a rider. Since beds are notoriously bad at staying in the proper lanes, there's a pusher at each corner. The rider, often a pajama-clad female with a good sense of direction, urges them on. The race is short but tricky. Teams have to maneuver a half-block straightaway followed by an obstacle course. "We don't tell what the obstacles will be from year to year because we don't want teams practicing up on them," said Hal Jensen, an event coordinator. In times past, the obstacles have included running with an egg in a spoon and the belly-to-belly football carry.

The races are held the second weekend after Labor Day, and proceeds go to the Flagstaff Toys for Tots program. Winners earn a chance to compete in a national competition at pro football's Super Bowl. For details on how to enter your box spring, log on to www.bedraceusa.com or call (877) 286–6095.

MIRACLE MOON'S MOTHERHOOD
North of Flagstaff

Miracle Moon is not only a white buffalo but also the world's most prolific producer of white buffalo. She was born on the plains of Wyoming. Her firstborn was also a white female and was named Rainbow Spirit. Since white-buffalo births occur with staggering infrequency, the birth was heralded as particularly rare.

But Miracle Moon wasn't done. She gave birth to Peace Pilgrim on July 18, 2001. Peace Pilgrim is also a female. A white female. Two in a row is so rare they don't even have statistics developed for it yet.

But there's more. The herd was moved to Arizona in December 2001, and on July 1, 2002, Miracle Moon delivered her third offspring. It was a male and it was also white. According to owners Jim and Dena Riley, the last white-male-buffalo birth in this country occurred more than fifty years ago. They named the new calf Arizona Spirit.

All four white buffalo have had their DNA tested three times to make sure they're purebreds, not a cross between buffalo and cattle. The Rileys say they did the testing because the white buffalo is sacred to some Indian tribes, and they wanted to make sure theirs were authentic.

The three white youngsters, their white mother, and their father, a normal-colored bull named Willie Wonka, are on display at Spirit Mountain Ranch, on Highway 180 about 20 miles north of Flagstaff. There's a fee for looking at them and another one for taking their picture. For more information, call (928) 606–2779 or log on to www.sacredwhitebuffalo.com.

THE FOUR-STATE CONTORTIONS
Four Corners

Most people say they visit the Four Corners National Monument because it's the only place in the country where four states meet. But what they really go there for is to have their picture taken while standing in four states at the same time. Because of that, it's a paradise for photographers who like to take pictures of people twisting themselves into weird shapes while looking at the camera and saying "cheese."

The four states meet at the intersection of a large X drawn in the center of a concrete slab. Through strategic placement of the arms and legs, visitors can stand in Arizona, Utah, Colorado, and New Mexico at the same time, then observe that weather conditions and the scenery in all four are pretty similar.

Most use the standard four-point squat, placing one foot and one hand in each state. The more adventuresome implement the quad-state plop, a technique in which they simply flop down over the X while flailing both arms and legs like a child making a snow angel.

Others have been observed making moves like those common to a singles' dance and the Twister game.

The monument is located on U.S. Route 160 in the far northeastern corner of Arizona

And the far southwestern corner of Colorado.

And the far southeastern corner of Utah.

And the far northwestern corner of New Mexico.

There's a nominal entry fee and once on the grounds, visitors may also purchase Navajo artifacts and food.

LEO, THE LOST LION

Charles Lindbergh once inadvertently caused a lion roundup by cowboys in the Mazatzal Mountains. In summer 1927, Metro-Goldwyn-Mayer Studios hired stunt-pilot Martin Jensen to fly the studio's trademark lion, Leo, on a nonstop flight from Los Angeles to New York. It was an effort to capitalize on the publicity surrounding Lindbergh's success, so the studio duplicated his plane, equipped it with a large cage, and loaded the 350-pound lion on board.

But the combined weight of the lion, cage, and extra fuel was too much for the B-1 Ryan Brougham plane, and it crashed in Hell's Gate Canyon on Tonto Creek. Neither Jensen nor Leo was injured, but there was no way the pilot could extricate the lion from the wreckage, so he set out on foot to find help. Almost four days later Jensen stumbled into a ranch house and told his story. After a night's rest he was taken to Payson, where he called for help.

In the meantime a couple of cowboys came across the downed plane and determined that the lion was weak but safe in the cage. They eventually led a search party to the crash site and Leo. The cowboys butchered a yearling calf, fed the lion, and then hauled him out of the canyon on a sled fashioned from the door of a small shed.

Leo stayed in Payson for a few days and was so popular that teachers dismissed school so the children could look at him, and then he was returned to California by truck. The incident generated substantial publicity for the studio bosses, but not the kind they wanted. And shortly after the crash, the Forest Service named the gulch where it happened Leo Canyon. It's still there, in the Tonto National Forest between Payson and Gisela. And it's still a tough place to find.

GOODWILL DINOSAURS
Holbrook

A couple of miles outside of Holbrook, the eastbound lanes of Interstate 40 go over a small rise. From that vantage point the landscape spreads out as gentle tan hills, scattered red rocks, and an azure sky that goes on forever. So one mile resembles the next and the stretch of road gets pretty boring.

Dinosaurs tear each other apart and snarf each other down in full view of passing traffic along Interstate 40 near Holbrook.

Except for the dinosaurs.

A whole herd of giant lizards stands right next to the free-way, ready to sink their humongous fangs into one of those snotty little sports cars or snarf down a loaded semi.

They're not real, of course, but they sure get your attention.

The dinosaurs are actually road signs, placed there to draw attention to the combined Dinosaur Park, International Petri-fied Forest, and Museum of the Americas, a tourist attraction. There are fourteen of the prehistoric beasts at present, with plans to add another twenty-six to the herd. Each is built of steel reinforcing rod and cement. Six stand guard over the free-way; the others are spread throughout the 6,500-acre park.

Visitors may also inspect petrified logs, a herd of live buf-falo, Native American pottery, actual dinosaur bones, and other remnants of times gone by. Or buy a dinosaur T-shirt.

The park is open seven days a week from dawn to dusk. But the dinosaurs never sleep. Really, really big-game hunters and Jurassic Park fans can get more information by calling (928) 524–9178.

NOT AN EASY SITDOWN
Holbrook

Elks Lodge 2450 bears resemblance to Elks lodges across the country. But one piece of decor sets 2450 apart from most others.

It's the elk-horn chair, a rather scary piece of furniture that looks like it might impale anyone brave enough to sit in it. Edward Leopold crafted it a long time ago from five and one-half sets of elk antlers, to sit outside the family establishment, the Pow Wow Trading Post and Motel in Holbrook.

Those who aren't afraid of punctured bottoms are welcome to take a seat
in the antler chair at the Elks Club in Holbrook.

After the elder Leopold died, the chair was passed on to his son, Ken, who used to sit in it and watch the tourists pass by. He later moved it to another motel and then, shortly before his death, requested that it be donated to the Elks lodge.

So now it sits in its own little room, beckoning those brave enough to risk being stabbed by an elk horn. "Sometimes the new officers sit in it and have their pictures taken for the newspaper," said Howard Fischer, a longtime lodge member. "But most of the time, it just sits there."

Waiting for its next victim.

The Holbrook Elks Lodge 2450 is located at 714 Elkdom Avenue. Interested in taking a seat? Call (928) 524–6789.

TEPEE FOR TWO OR THREE OR MORE
Holbrook

The Wigwam Motel is a place where memories are born. John Lewis, one of the current owners, says he gets inquiries from people all over the nation, wondering if the establishment is still there. And when he replies that it is, the callers often get teary-eyed remembering the first time they stayed there. "It's a place you don't forget," Lewis explained.

The motel has fifteen individual units, each shaped like a tepee. Built by Chester Lewis, John's father, it opened in 1950, and each tepee still has its original furniture, including two full-size beds. There's also a television set, capable of receiving fifty channels off of cable. But, as a sign of respect for the past, there are no phones.

The wigwams are 21 feet in diameter. And, of course, they're better built than the real wigwams, which were made of lodge

The Wigwam Motel in Holbrook has been a place to sleep in the round since the 1950s.

poles and animal hide. These tepees are lumber, tar paper, chicken wire, and stucco. "We get some strong winds up here," Lewis said, "but we've never had one blow down."

The Wigwam shut down in late 1970, then reopened in 1988 to keep its mission of creating memories on a nightly basis.

It's located on the corner of Hopi Drive and Eighth Avenue. If you want to sleep in the round, call (800) 414–3021.

ONE WAY TO STOP THIEVES
Joseph City

The folks at Geronimo Indian Store don't have to worry about anybody walking off with their prize attraction. Most people aren't capable of picking up a 45-ton rock. Even if they did find enough cranes, bulldozers, front-end loaders, and winches to haul it away, then what'd they do with it? Hide it in a dresser drawer at home? Put it in a safety-deposit box until the statute of limitations expires? Probably not. So the World's Largest Petrified Tree appears to be safe. At least until a spaceship comes along and beams it up for scientific study.

The tree is a humongous thing, weighing in at about 89,000 pounds, a factor that holds pilferage to a minimum. Elvera Wiegand, an employee at the Indian Store, says she's not sure of the total weight but offers the inside information that the trunk weighs 168 pounds per cubic foot, if that makes figuring any easier.

Owner Carl Kempton dug it up from a gravel pit behind the store, moved it to his parking lot, and buried part of it in a 4-foot hole. Only about 8 feet of the root section is aboveground, but that's enough to create a photo opportunity. Several other smaller petrified logs surround the centerpiece. Kempton believes they're all from the same tree, which measured more than 100 feet when it was still alive back in the days before chain saws and gift shops.

The store and old log are at the Geronimo exit off Interstate 40, about 5 miles west of Holbrook.

ROCK ART CANYON
Joseph City

S everal years ago Brantley Baird figured that raising cows wasn't going to provide him with the lifestyle he wanted. So he turned to petroglyphs as a primary source of income.

It wasn't real difficult. His family owns 7,300 acres of what used to be the Hashknife Ranch, a legendary spread that once covered two million acres and was home to as many as 60,000 cows at a time. The most outstanding feature of Baird's property is a canyon filled with ancient rock drawings.

There's something about rock drawings (petroglyphs) that fascinates people, so Baird decided to capitalize on it. In 1995, in the middle of a slump in cattle prices and a drought, he quit herding cattle and took up ramrodding tourists.

Now he takes as many as thirty visitors at a time to his canyon and explains, in his good-ol'-boy twang, that "these petroglyphs, some of 'em, go back as far as 7,000 years. I can't verify that personally, of course. I'm just repeating what the archaeologists tell me."

Although their respective ages total almost 150 years, Baird and his foreman, Clem T. Rogers, built a road to the canyon, an observation deck overlooking the canyon, and a staircase to the bottom so the tourists can get a close-up look at something that's even older than Brantley and Clem.

The Rock Art Ranch is open to tourists daily except for Sundays and major holidays. Directions and reservations are mandatory. If you want to talk to Brantley, call him at (928) 288–3260.

You Want History with That Whopper?
Kayenta

During World War II and for many years afterwards, the Navajo Code Talkers were a well-kept secret despite the fact that they played a major role in the defeat of the Japanese. Since their language was unwritten at the time, Navajo soldiers were used to pass orders to officers without fear of the messages being decoded by the enemy.

Now the Code Talkers are being honored in many ways. A large sculpture memorializes them in downtown Phoenix, they were the subjects of the 2002 movie *Wind Talkers,* and their story is also recounted in the Burger King here. Richard Mike, owner of the franchise, created a display of wartime mementos brought home by his father, King Paul Mike, who served as a Code Talker.

The cases hold little bits and pieces of the war from the Navajo perspective, including photographs of "the women who were left behind," Japanese flags, and military equipment from both sides.

There is no charge to view the exhibit. The Burger King is located on U.S. Route 160 as it passes through Kayenta on the Navajo Indian Reservation.

A Night in an Octagon
Kinlichee

There are people who don't mind sleeping on the floor with only a sheepskin separating them from the bare earth, people who can function where there's no electricity or plumbing and their cell phones don't work. For them, there is the hogan of Clarissa Williams.

She is the operator of the family hogan, a traditional eight-sided dwelling that has been converted into a bed-and-breakfast known as the Two White Rocks Hospitality. Visitors get to spend nights with only a kerosene lantern for light and a trip into yesteryear if they have to use the bathroom. But they can also enjoy spectacular views in the daytime, learn the ancient art of rug weaving, listen to a Navajo storyteller, take a guided hike through the nearby sandstone formations, and take part in a purification ceremony in an authentic sweat lodge.

The hogan is a symbolic structure built of logs and a dirt roof and used only for sleeping. The meals are prepared in an adjacent cabin by family members. "There's only one place on the property where the cell phone works," Williams said, "and you have to know exactly where it is to get a signal. We call that spot the Phone Booth." Despite the lack of modern conveniences, guests seeking a Native American experience regularly occupy the hogan and several others like it on the Navajo Reservation.

For information, call Clarissa Williams at (928) 871–4360, or the Navajo Nation Visitors Center, (928) 871–6436.

THE LURE OF THE LURES
Payson

Ken Gouker readily admits he's hooked and blames it all on his wife, Jean. She made him go along with her to all those yard sales on that fateful day more than twenty years ago. "I bought an old box full of fishing equipment and found the lures," he said. "I got excited and started looking for more." As a result, Gouker collects fishing lures; he now has so many they take up a substantial portion of the house.

Ken Gouker of Payson is also known as "Baitman." He has enough fishing lures to empty a lake, but he never uses them to catch fish because they're too valuable.

He said he's not sure how many he owns but estimated the total to be in the thousands. "There's more than 650 in that one display case alone," he said. The display case is the focal point of the couple's living room. He also has tackle boxes and wall displays filled with lures that are a multitude of colors and shapes and vary in length from less than an inch to more than a foot.

But none of them will ever get wet. Fishing-lure collectors pursue their quarry strictly for ownership, not for utilitarian reasons. Besides, every lure he owns is from a discontinued line, so it will never be reproduced and that makes it more valuable. He is a regular at national fishing-lure conventions, where he buys, sells, and trades. In addition, he never misses a yard sale. Further, his personalized license plate reads BAIT-MAN. And his wife's says BAITGAL.

Gouker does fish but not with his trophy lures. He buys the cheaper kind so if one gets caught on a sunken log, he can cut it off without fear of losing a fortune. If the allure of the lure is your thing, you can probably find a soul mate by calling Ken at (928) 474-5203.

THE CURSE OF THE STONE
Petrified Forest National Park

Signs throughout Petrified Forest National Park warn visitors not to remove pieces of petrified wood, not even the tiny little ones just lying there on the ground. The fines are stiff, up to $275 for taking just a sliver, but even worse is The Curse.

An exhibit at the Rainbow Forest Museum, which serves as a visitor center at the south end of the park, is filled with testimonials from petty thieves, rock hounds, and others who made off with some of the pieces. Many of the testimonials deal with the problems that followed the crimes.

"I am returning the rock and the bad luck that followed it," wrote one penitent. "Since I have had it, my bike has been stolen and my feet had blisters as big as my hand. And I know my side hurts and it might be a hurnea and worse of all me and my girlfriend are about to brake up . . . "

Another tortured soul confessed, "(We) smuggled out three small pieces of petrified wood, carefully stuck inside a bra on the body. That evening our bad luck began. One person had stomach cramps and diarrhea . . . that same night we were the only ones to be attacked by flying ants in the campground."

Park rangers say they receive two or three packets containing misappropriated petrified wood every week. Sometimes the returned rocks come from family members ashamed of what their kinfolk did. This one, for example:

"I don't know what possessed my father to take a piece of wood . . . to this day I remember him placing it in a pack of cigarettes . . . it was a part of my rock collection as a child but even then I knew it was wrong."

But for many others the price was higher than guilt. Here's an example:

"Not known to me, my husband took several fossils from the park. Bad luck has plagued us ever since. His mother and my mother died, and my cousin, who was also my best friend, died. My husband had an affair . . . later he lost his job and we became financially strapped. . . and (he) became a hard-drinking stranger. Please accept these cursed fossils with my blessing."

The Petrified Forest National Park is located off Interstate 40 east of Holbrook. For details on The Curse and other matters, call (928) 524–6228. And remember, take only pictures.

A SCRAP-IRON ARTIST
Pine

Tony Roberson turns metal files into snakes and uses horse-shoes to make chairs. An occupation like that requires special tools that aren't available anymore, neither at the hardware store nor from a mail-order catalog, so Roberson either makes his own equipment or buys it from antique dealers. His workshop is filled with century-old vises and forges, ancient anvils, and stacks of broken axles and rusted iron rods. "They're not junk," he said. "They're my tools."

Roberson started as a blacksmith's helper when he was ten years old and said he's one of only sixty smiths left in Arizona. Because the ranks are dwindling, blacksmithing tools are becoming rare, forcing him to make his own from those broken axles and rusted iron rods.

Although capable of performing the common blacksmith jobs, Roberson concentrates on the vocation as an art form. In a forge he built himself, he heats a farrier's rasp to 2,000 degrees Fahrenheit and hammers it into a rattlesnake. Old horseshoes are recycled as door knockers and toilet-paper holders; flatware becomes key rings and an iron rod is fashioned into a meat turner.

Some of his work is larger. More than one hundred horse-shoes went into the creation of a bench and accompanying chairs. But, although he uses horseshoes extensively in his work, Roberson said he is not a farrier. "You won't catch me trying to put a shoe on a 1,200 pound animal," he joked.

His shop, Lone Wolf Blacksmith, is located in one of the oldest buildings in Pine. It's on State Route 87, and it's open when he's there and closed when he's not. Those who simply have to have a horseshoe sofa can call (928) 978-9240.

Hawkeye Feed and Rodeo Supply in Lakeside has changed ownership, but the big egg always stays on the roof. Former owner Lori Vivolo says she never once considered making it into an omelet.

S *LIGHTLY* E *GGCENTRIC*
P *inetop - L a k e s i d e*

H awkeye Feed and Rodeo Supply is housed in a 1-story red
building that would be easy to miss if a big egg wasn't sitting on top of it. This eggcelent eggsample of rustic art was
placed on the roof thirty years ago and stands nearly 10 feet tall
and about 4 feet in diameter. (These are not eggzact figures.)

John Bailey, the original owner of the store, crafted the egg
from fiberglass, slapped a cowboy hat on it, and perched it atop
his place of business. It's been there ever since, even though the
establishment has changed ownership.

Lori Vivolo, who owned the store in summer 2002, said,
"people sometimes forget the name, but everybody remembers
the egg."

And just so you don't have an eggscuse for not stopping in
the next time you're in Lakeside, the egg (and the store) is
located at 3002 White Mountain Boulevard. Don't worry. You
won't get overeggzerted looking for it.

A S *EAT* FOR F *ORTY* (*OR* M *ORE*)
P *inetop - L a k e s i d e*

K aren Meyer said the big chair out in front was supposed to
attract attention. It does.

It's not the design. The chair is similar to many others sold
at home-decoration shops in the tall pines—made of wood and
made to look rustic. Where it differs is in the size. This one is

The big chair in front of Wild Woods in Pinetop was built as a tourist attraction, and it works, according to co-owner Karen Meyer.

nearly 15 feet tall and 8 feet across, so it has room for an entire convention of rear ends.

Curt Meyer, Karen's husband, builds all the furniture for their home-furnishing and accessory store. So when the couple needed an attention getter, he used pine logs to construct a chair that can hold Mom, Pop, Junior, Sister, Aunt Maude, Uncle Harry, and three neighbor kids. In fact a local business put about forty employees in and around the chair for a group photo.

"It's really popular around Christmas because people put their children on the seat and take a picture," Karen Meyer said.

People who like lots of derriere room will find the chair at Wild Woods, 2314 East White Mountain Boulevard in Pinetop.

It's a Rye Humor
Rye

R on Adler says he likes to make people smile. But sometimes, when they visit All Bikes, his two-acre lot filled with old frames and wheels, they break down in tears. "There's just something about seeing your first bike again," he explained. "A bike is your first sense of freedom. You're not with your mom and dad anymore. You're on your own."

Adler's collection of Monarchs, Schwinns, Whizzers, and Black Phantoms marches across his hillside property like an army of circular steel and chrome. From the road they look like they've been dumped there and left to rot, but there's actually some organization among the rows. Only Adler himself, however, knows the key to where everything is.

He claims he has no idea how many he has. "If you really have to know," he said, "you'll have to count them yourself." The offer has never been accepted, but a quick estimate indicates the figure is in the thousands. Adler and eight semi-trailers loaded with bikes moved to Rye in 1988. His sells parts and entire two-wheelers to customers all over the world.

A hand-painted sign in front of the business says there's also a museum on the premises, but it needs work. In its present form it's merely a covered area where old bikes hang from the rafters. But it's free.

Ron Adler deals in memories and old
bicycles on his acreage near Rye.

All Bikes is on State Route 87 in downtown Rye and is open from 9:00 A.M. to 6:00 P.M. Wednesdays through Sundays. Those interested in a Schwinn-or-lose encounter can call (928) 474–2526.

NAMED BY THE TURN OF A CARD
Show Low

T wo old bronze cowboys play an eternal card game in a downtown park here as a perpetual reminder that the community got its name from a gambling incident.

It was back in the late 1800s. Marion Clark and Corydon E. Cooley were partners who homesteaded a 100,000-acre ranch. But they had a falling out and decided to dissolve their partnership with a card game called Seven Up. Under the rules of the game, the winner would buy out the loser. According to local lore the game went on through the night and on the last hand, Clark allegedly said, "You show low and you win." Cooley cut the deck and came up with the two of clubs, thus winning the game and the option to buy the land that eventually became Show Low.

In recognition of the feat, the town's main street has been named Deuce of Clubs while two other thoroughfares bear the names of Cooley and Clark. The bronze sculpture in the park depicts the pair at the gambling table just as Cooley turned the deuce.

It could have been worse. Suppose they'd been playing poker. Then the town might have been named something like Two Twos. Or Stud. Or Flush.

For more information on how to acquire land with deuces, call the Show Low Regional Chamber of Commerce at (928) 537–2326 or check out www.showlowchamberofcommerce.com.

GOLF IN THE SADDLE
Springerville

Even though Tiger Woods and Sergio Garcia have never heard of it, cow pasture golf is so popular in this area that folks not only hold a tournament, they hold two tournaments, one in June and one in September. The sport, introduced to Arizona in 1996, is similar to regular golf with some notable exceptions. For one thing, golfers have to tee up on a cow pie on the first hole. So instead of making a *whack* when club meets ball and cow pie, it's more of a *smoosh.*

And replacing a divot requires an exceptionally delicate touch.

(It should be pointed out that cowboy golfers ride horses between shots but dismount before hitting the ball. That, and the uniforms, sets cowboy golf apart from polo.)

The courses are only nine holes, but they're filled with hoof prints. Cows are a vital part of cowboy golf because they keep the fairways trimmed. Whenever it rains, however, the cows go nutso. They get to stomping and schmoozing and pretty soon the whole pasture is filled with holes caused by the cows sinking in clear up to where their ankles would be if cows had ankles.

The greens are also tough. There's no bent grass or tiff grass, only cow-pasture grass, some of it 6 inches tall. And since cows don't know the difference between greens and fairways, they also stomp all over the greens, leaving footprints and cow plops with equal enthusiasm. This makes it extremely difficult to read the breaks.

To compensate, the holes are cut larger than on regular courses. Most are coffee cans sunk into the ground on the easy holes and hula hoops on the tougher mountainside greens. Cowboy golfers are also limited in club selection because they can carry only as many clubs as will fit into the cutoff leg of a pair of blue jeans, which serve as golf bags.

Lastly, cowboy-golf terminology is also different. When regular golfers want a ball to stop on the green, they yell, "Bite!" Among cowboy golfers the proper phrase is, "Whoa back thar, you li'l varmint!"

Those interested in subjecting themselves to this type of entertainment can call the Round Valley Chamber of Commerce at (928) 333–2123, or the X-Diamond Ranch at (928) 333–2286.

ALIEN ABDUCTION OR HOAX?

On November 5, 1975, a group of loggers in the White Mountains allegedly saw an unusually bright light in the forest. One of the men, Travis Walton, ran toward the light and, according to witnesses, was zapped by a bolt of energy. The others in the work crew panicked and sped off in their pickup truck. After reporting the incident to authorities, they returned to the scene. But Walton had disappeared.

Five days later Walton called his brother from a phone booth in a nearby community. Later he claimed to have been abducted by aliens "with huge, luminous brown eyes the size of quarters." His story attracted national attention, and a verbal battle raged over his credibility. There were charges of fixed polygraph tests and accusations that the incident had been staged to make money by selling the tale to the tabloids.

But Walton stuck to his story and wrote a book about the experience. In 1993 Paramount Pictures released Fire in the Sky, a movie based on the book, starring James Garner as a local lawman. Although the media hype about the movie claimed it would answer all the unanswered questions, it did little to settle the issue.

And now, almost thirty years later, there are still widely divergent opinions on the entire matter. There's a whole lot more information about it on the Internet. Start with www.travis-walton.com/ and check the connecting links.

ATHLETES FROM OUTER SPACE?
Springerville

There's no other way to put this: The athletic field where Round Valley High School students perform looks like a flying saucer.

Technically it's an ensphere, which is another word for "dome." It is quite large, enclosing 8 million cubic feet and providing a field area of 113,000 square feet. It's so big that if they want to, school officials can stage three basketball games or two soccer games at the same time.

The dome was erected (or landed) more than a decade ago, opening in October 1992 at a cost of $11.7 million. It can hold 10,000 fans who watch football, basketball, track and field, tennis, badminton, soccer, volleyball, Special Olympics, and concerts. It's a very versatile place. For example, the artificial turf that covers the football field can be removed and replaced with wooden basketball flooring.

It was the first enclosed high-school football field in the nation. It is fully lit by sunlight in the daytime, and the sunlight also heats the facility.

The students come from Springerville, Eagar, Alpine, Greer, and Nutrioso. They call their teams the Round Valley High School Elks and resist outsider suggestions that they should be known as the Aliens. Or the Spacemen. Or the UFO Pilots.

For information on how to rent the hall, contact dome director Tom Pifer at (928) 333–5677.

BUILDER, SPARE THAT TREE
Strawberry

The north side of the lobby in the Strawberry Lodge is disrupted by a peculiar stone semicircle that runs from floor to ceiling. It was put there to save a tree.

When Jean and Richard Turner bought the lodge in 1967, they undertook a major rebuilding project that would include the addition of eight guest rooms, a restaurant, and a lobby. But there was a problem—there was a tree growing right where they wanted to put the lobby. And it wasn't just any old tree; it was an old oak tree that, according to local folklore, had been living on that spot for more than 200 years. "We couldn't cut it down," Jean Turner said. "Oh, no. It was too fine a tree for that."

Rather than scuttle their building plans, the Turners opted to circumvent the tree. They used rock from their mining claim to erect the semicircle, and then built the room around it. This resulted in an odd-looking lobby and made it difficult to find suitable furniture. But all in all, the end result fits in well with the lodge's rustic decor.

The tree-saving effort is more noticeable on the outside, where the builders left plenty of space between the tree and the lodge in case the oak wasn't done growing.

The lodge is on the west side of State Route 87 as it passes through downtown Strawberry. Arborists and anyone else seeking information should call (928) 476–3333.

JOHN SHAW'S
LAST SNORT

*A*lthough it happened almost a century ago, the story of John Shaw keeps popping up as a reminder that some of those tales of the Wild and Wooly West were actually true.

Shaw was a minor-league thief who made the mistake of teaming with an accomplice to rob a dice game being held in a Winslow tavern. They got away, but only as far as Canyon Diablo, a foreboding place located some 20 miles west of Winslow. There, a sheriff's posse caught up with them and a gunfight ensued. The accomplice was wounded, but Shaw took a fatal bullet. Once they determined he was finally dead, posse members unceremoniously dumped his body into a shallow grave and departed.

But back at the tavern, someone remembered that Shaw had paid for a drink and never received it. For a reason nobody could remember, this spurred some sense of justice among the patrons. So a bunch of them boarded the next train to Two Guns, where they disembarked, dug up Shaw's body, and poured a snort of whiskey down his throat.

The event was recorded for posterity by one of the loyal barflies who brought along a camera and took a picture of the corpse being held up by several former drinking companions.

THE TOTEM MONUMENT
Strawberry

Most monuments are sculptures cast in bronze or carved in stone, but here among the pines there stands a totem pole dedicated to Ernest Ralls, a member of the citizenry. Even though Arizona is noted for its Indian art, the totem pole looks a little out of place because totems are commonly associated with tribes in Canada and Alaska.

But this one is here because Ralls always wanted a totem pole. So he hired Arizona wood-carver John Quick to create one from a tree killed by lightning. It stands about 25 feet tall and features a bear, a frog, and an eagle.

After Ralls died, neighbors and relatives dedicated the totem to his memory and had a plaque installed near the base. It reads: IN GRATITUDE OF ERNEST R. RALLS JR., MARCH 14, 1920–DECEMBER 14, 1998, FOR THE CREATIVE PLANNING, LOVE, DEDICA-TION, AND BEAUTIFICATION OF THIS AREA.

The memorial totem watches over Fossil Creek Road about 1.25 miles west of State Route 87 in Strawberry.

When he was alive, Ernest Ralls always wanted a totem pole, so he had one carved. Now, after his death, it stands as his memorial near Strawberry.

A City in the Sky
Walpi

For those who are interested in time travel but can't afford one of those fancy Jules Verne machines, the village of Walpi on the Hopi Reservation has a definite back-in-time atmosphere. It sits atop a large mesa and there's only one road leading to it, so the community is isolated from the rest of the world. There's no electricity or running water, and many of the houses are made of native stone that was hauled to the site by the people who lived there 200 years ago.

The edges of the mesa drop off sharply and the road narrows to 15 feet as it enters Walpi, so the only vehicles allowed are owned by residents who know how to maneuver the territory without falling off. Visitors are allowed, but they must walk. Before they walk, however, they have to make arrangements with an authorized Hopi guide. Once there the guests may purchase kachina dolls and pottery crafted by the inhabitants.

There's a serenity about the village but if you go there, be forewarned that photography is forbidden on the entire Hopi Reservation, and the rule is strictly enforced in Walpi and on the other mesas. So resist the urge to snap off just one shot while nobody's looking. If you don't, you might have your camera confiscated.

Walpi is located off State Route 264 near Polacca. For information, call (928) 737-2262.

GREETINGS FROM GORT
Whispering Pines

G ort was a robot, one of several assigned to patrol Earth by disgusted spacemen who didn't like the way humans were messing up the universe in the 1951 sci-fi movie *The Day the Earth Stood Still.* The robots were very powerful and designed to act as a police force.

Since the movie was fiction, there are no actual Gorts overseeing the earthlings. But facsimiles pop up occasionally. There's one in Rex Donley's front yard. It stands about 15 feet high. This makes it rather frightening but in a whimsical way, because this Gort's head is a wind turbine and the body is made of air-conditioning ducts.

Donley, who describes himself as a handyman with artistic leanings, built the thing at the

Rex Donley admits he has too much time on his hands, so he makes things like Gort, a giant ductwork sculpture.

urging of his son and installed Christmas tree lights inside so the head glows at night. The robot is not his only artistic endeavor, however. His yard is also home to a windmill made of railroad spikes, bowling ball wind chimes, and an airplane built completely of logs.

Believers in the true Gort, bowling artisans, and log-plane enthusiasts can find Donley's place by taking Houston Mesa Road off State Route 87 on the north end of Payson. Follow Houston Mesa Road for about 11 miles and turn right just after crossing the creek. It's the first house on the right. And remember to say "Gort! Klaatu barada nikto" so you don't get zapped.

AN AUDIBLE VORTEX
Window Rock

The Navajo Museum, Library and Visitors Center is a beautiful structure designed to preserve the culture and beliefs of the tribal members. It has galleries that feature the work of Navajo artists, an extensive library well equipped with computers, an auditorium, conference rooms, and a gift shop.

But as spectacular as the museum itself is, there's something even more interesting in the outdoor amphitheater located near the entrance. It's a large concrete circle with a raised concrete platform in the middle. Two indented lines divide the platform, cutting it into equal quarters.

And here's where it gets interesting. If you stand directly where the two lines intersect and speak in a normal tone, your voice reverberates inside your head, like it did when you were a kid and put a five-gallon plastic bucket over your head so your voice would echo back.

Then it gets even weirder. Although your voice is making loud noises inside your own head, it sounds normal to anyone listening to you. They can be only a few feet away and won't notice anything different.

And now this is where it gets really strange—if you step just 6 inches off the intersection of the two quartering lines, there's no reverberation when you speak. Step back onto the X and it comes back. Step off, and it's gone again. It works every time. Trust me on this one.

Kathy Curley, marketing coordinator for Navajo Nation Tourism, said there's no scientific explanation for it. "But the tribal medicine men say it's a spiritual place," she shared.

The museum is on State Route 264 on the east edge of Window Rock. Admission is free.

FINALLY, A CORNER FOR STANDIN' ON WINSLOW

For a long time, people would come to Winslow just to stand on a corner. Problem was, they were never sure which corner to stand on. But thanks to some farsighted people who know how corner-standers like to have a place of their own, the dilemma has been resolved. Now there is an official Standin' On a Corner in Winslow Arizona Park in Winslow, Arizona.

All this came about because of a line in the song "Take It Easy," written by Jackson Browne and Glenn Frey and recorded by the Eagles. It refers to a young man who was standin' on a corner in Winslow when a girl in a flatbed Ford slows down to look him over.

As parks go, this one isn't much, size wise. It's only 30 feet wide and 134 feet long. So there's room enough for only a couple of trees, some old-fashioned lampposts, and a minimal amount of grass, because most of the ground is covered with the engraved bricks that helped raise money for the project.

There's finally a corner for standin' on for those music fans who always wanted to stand on a corner in Winslow, Arizona, like it says in the song.

It was built on the site of an old drugstore that was destroyed by fire. An adjacent building remained, so it became the west boundary of the park. The bare bricks and mortar are covered by a mural depicting an image of that girl in a flatbed truck reflected in the window of a motel. And in the foreground, leaning on his guitar and looking like he wants to be looked at, is a life-size bronze statue of the young man who came to Winslow to stand on a corner.

The citizens of Winslow who first proposed such a park were warned that they'd be the laughingstock of the state if they went ahead with the idea. They went ahead anyway, and now hundreds of tourists get off Interstate 40 every week to come here and stand on a corner.

The park is located at the corner of Kinsley Avenue and Second Street, which was once part of the fabled Route 66. Anyone can go there, and there's no fee for standing.

A SEATING SAGA
Winslow

Mary Jane Colter's benches are back at La Posada, but it took a court order to get them there.

Colter, one of the nation's foremost female architects, was hired by the Fred Harvey Company to design buildings along the Santa Fe Railroad line and at the Grand Canyon. Her favorite was La Posada, built here in 1929 as a train station and hotel.

She structured the building to utilize the wind as a cooling agent and incorporated ample seating for the weary passengers by personally designing a series of wooden benches.

La Posada's days as a fine hotel ended in 1957, and it was converted into office space for the railroad. It was scheduled for demolition in 1994, but a group of determined citizens banded together to save it through the acquisition of federal grants. They were successful and eventually the property was sold to Californian Allan Affeldt, who began a major restoration.

While working with Colter's original plans, Affeldt came across drawings for the benches. He learned Amtrak, then the owner of the hotel, had moved them to the train station in Flagstaff in the early 1970s. Flagstaff, Winslow, and the station in Flagstaff then went through an extended battle to determine ownership before some higher power said they belonged back at the hotel.

Later a Winslow contingent composed of football players and flatbed trucks arrived in Flagstaff to lay claim to their prize, but no one told the Amtrak ticket agent about the decision. He called the cops and the shouting match that followed had to be settled by the mayor.

Eventually the hostage benches were released to their rightful owners and returned to La Posada's elegant lobby, where they await the behinds of those who pass by.

La Posada is located between Route 66 and the railroad tracks in downtown Winslow. For seating information, call (928) 289–4366.

NEW USE FOR OLD LOGS
Winslow

Peter Wolf Toth arrived in Winslow in 1979, intent on adding one of his artworks to the city's landscape. All he asked for was a log and a place to put it. When he left four months later, there was a 30-foot-tall Indian head doing sentry duty over the community.

Artist Peter Wolf Toth left this legacy in Winslow—a 30-foot Indian head carved from a single log.

Toth's family fled Communist-controlled Hungary in the 1960s and settled in Ohio. While in college Toth became interested in American Indians and what he considered the inhumane treatment they had received from settlers and the federal government. So he set out to make a statement of protest by carving fifty huge Indian heads, one in every state. He started in California, then moved back east, spending four to six months in each of the selected cities.

His Arizona project, carved from a 30-foot ponderosa-pine log, was the thirty-third in his series, which he called "The Trail of the Whispering Giants." The artist applied about a hundred coats of preservative to the finished sculpture, which still stands where he left it, on a man-made hill next to the visitor center in northeast Winslow. The wood shows a couple of splits but overall, the piece has withstood the ravages of time and temperature very well.

Toth, incidentally, successfully completed his mission by carving similar statues in every state. There's no charge for looking at any of them. The Winslow artwork is located at 300 West North Street. Take exit 253 off I–40 and go north.

INVITATION TO A HANGING
Winslow

Once upon a time there was a sheriff who tried to do a fun thing, but he should have taken a correspondence course in execution etiquette. It happened in Navajo County when a man was sentenced to death by hanging for the murder of a coworker.

The law required witnesses at the execution, so it was up to Sheriff Frank Wattron to take care of the guest list. He had invitations printed and mailed, but his choice of wording got him in big trouble. The invitation read:

"You are hereby cordially invited to attend the hanging of one George Smiley, Murderer. His soul will be swung into eternity on December 8, 1899, at 2 o'clock P.M., sharp. Latest improved methods in the art of strangulation will be employed and everything possible will be done to make the surroundings cheerful and the execution a success."

Within days the contents of the invitation became national news. President William McKinley expressed outrage and chastised the sheriff, who was also condemned by newspapers across the territory. The furor forced postponement of the hanging and Wattron was obliged to write another invitation. This one said the execution would be held "with profound sorrow and regret" and that "conduct bordering on ribaldry would not be tolerated." Smiley was hanged on January 8, 1900.

The last remaining original invitation is on display at the Old Trails Museum, 212 Kinsley Avenue in Winslow, which also exhibits other items of historical significance and interest. For more information, call (928) 289–5861.

A HAREY RIDE
Winslow

It may not be the world's largest jackrabbit or even the world's heaviest jackrabbit, but the gray hare that hunkers outside the Jackrabbit Trading Post is probably the world's most-sat-upon jackrabbit. Every camera-toter who passes this way is almost obligated to take a photo of friend or family member perched on the big bunny's back.

The rabbit is a direct descendant of the first hare used to advertise the trading post. That one was a crouching black

Tony Jaquez owns both the Jackrabbit Trading Post
and the huge rabbit that gives it character. They're
on Jackrabbit Road east of Winslow.

creature that just got worn out by tourists, so the owner at the time found the replacement, a huge hare that was originally scheduled for placement in an amusement park. The silhouette of the first bunny is still used on all the signage along Interstate 40, and that's what draws many people to the store, according to current owner Tony Jaquez.

The newest claimant to the jackrabbit throne stands about 9 feet tall (including ears) and is outfitted with a saddle for easier mounting and riding. After the photo shoots, visitors are readily welcomed inside the trading post to browse, sample the cherry cider, and buy stuff.

The store is located south of I–40 at exit 269, about 12 miles east of Winslow.

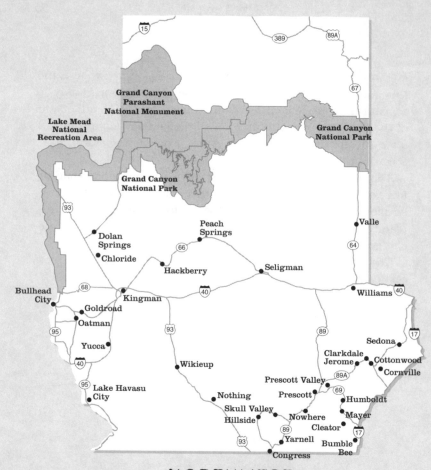

Grand Canyon
Parashant
National Monument

Lake Mead
National
Recreation Area

Grand Canyon
National Park

Grand Canyon
National Park

Valle

Peach
Springs

Dolan
Springs

Chloride

Hackberry

Seligman

Williams

Bullhead
City

Kingman

Goldroad

Oatman

Yucca

Wikieup

Sedona

Clarkdale
Jerome

Cottonwood

Cornville

Prescott Valley

Lake Havasu
City

Nothing

Prescott

Humboldt

Skull Valley

Nowhere

Mayer

Hillside

Cleator

Yarnell

Bumble
Bee

Congress

NORTHWEST

NORTHWEST

THERE'S NO BULL IN BULLHEAD
Bullhead City

Since Bullhead City borders the Colorado River, and since the
Colorado River often produces fish so big that those who
reel them in don't even have to lie about their size, it's only natural to assume that the town's name comes from the bullhead,
a species of fish that thrives in almost any water.

Not so. The bullhead in this instance is a huge rock that,
when gazed upon at the right angle in just the proper light,
resembles a horned bull, a species of animal that thrives anywhere it darn well pleases. The rock sat in the middle of the
river and became such an important symbol for the area that
when it came time to pick a town name, the bull's-head rock
was an obvious choice.

But then in the 1930s, the Bureau of Reclamation built
Parker Dam, which backed up the Colorado's waters to form
Lake Havasu. So now the namesake of Bullhead City lies
beneath the lake, and there's no way of rescuing it. There's
some bar talk now and then about building a cofferdam around
the bull to make it visible. Or sending divers down to find the
rock, then installing a series of underwater lights around it.
But when the beer runs out, nobody remembers exactly where
the rock is. Besides that, the water depth reaches as much as
200 feet, making volunteer divers and dam builders hard to
come by.

So the common philosophy here is to let underwater bulls lie.

READIN' 'N' RITIN' 'N' TRADIN'
Bumble Bee

There are a couple of amazing things related to Bumble Bee. One is that it's still on the map, considering it has a permanent population of two. The other is that the Bumble Bee Trading Post is not only open, but also thriving. At least on weekends.

The building was originally a schoolhouse, built in 1936. Bumble Bee was a mining town on the main road between Phoenix and Prescott, but it was bypassed by a freeway and fell into ghost-town status. Jerry and Elissa Fulton bought the school in 1979 and converted it into a combination residence and trading post. They used a lot of salvage during the reconstruction—the ceiling beams came from mines and bridges, the fences are narrow-gauge railroad tracks, and some of the door frames were once box springs.

Jerry Fulton died in 1998, but Elissa stayed on and operates the trading post with a new partner, Virgil George. Their trading is sort of a barter system: Visitors give them cash or credit-card numbers in trade for food, Native American kachinas and pottery, and stuff not common to big-city stores, such as necklaces made of rattlesnake vertebrae. The post is open only Friday through Sunday and even though it's located at the end of a winding, bumpy dirt road, the guest book lists visitors from Europe, Asia, and South America.

There are two versions of how the place got its name. One is that soldiers said the Indians in the area were "as thick as bumble bees." The other says prospectors named it after bees attacked them when they tried to remove honey from a hive. Now the trading post's motto is, "You'll Never Get Stung at Bumble Bee Trading Post."

The post is north of Phoenix, 5 miles west of Interstate 17 at exit 248. Virgil warns that reservations are required for "a really good meal at a reasonable price." Call (623) 374–5426. Or check out their Web site, www.bumblebeetradingpost.com.

A r t   o n   t h e   R o c k s
C h l o r i d e

I n these parts the painted rocks of Chloride are simply known as "the mural." Roy Purcell, the artist, calls the work *The Journey* and says it was the result of deep personal introspection. Either way, the rocks have withstood the elements, bureaucracy, and the streams of tourists who travel the crooked mile to view them, photograph them, comment on them, and attempt to decipher their hidden meanings.

The mural is both huge and hard to reach. The granite boulders that served as Purcell's canvas rise 75 feet above the canyon floor, and some of the painted figures are life-size times four. The road to the canyon can easily turn the family car into a $750 repair bill. Tour buses can't go there because the trail resembles a path left by a giant serpent suffering from the hiccups.

Purcell was working as a miner in 1966 when he came across the big rocks and decided to convert them into objets d'art. Another miner grubstaked the project by paying for supplies and rounding up some cronies to build scaffolding. Purcell used automobile paint so the colors are still vibrant.

While applying paint to rock one day, Purcell was ordered to stop his work by Bureau of Land Management agents. "I didn't bother to find out who owned the land," he said years later. "So I stopped and ate lunch. They left and I went back to work. They didn't say how long I was supposed to stop. I never heard from them again."

Chloride is about 15 miles north of Kingman off U.S. Highway 93. The mural is 1.3 miles southeast of the community. Follow the signs on the main street. The road is dirt and difficult but not impassable. Take your time. Those rocks have been there for millions of years. They're not going anywhere.

THE RETURN OF THE FULL SERVICEMAN
Clarkdale

In a world frantically driven to computerize and modernize all things, it's still possible to run across sentinels standing guard at the doorways of time to make sure we don't forget our yesterdays. One is the Clarkdale Classic Station on the corner of Main Street.

Although old, it has the ability to transport visitors backward in time, returning them to the days when going to the service station was almost pleasant, not a get-out-and-gas-it-up necessity. The reason is that it's a full-service station, one of the very few left in the country.

The station was constructed in 1938; current owner Michael Hensley bought it in 1989 and began restoring it. "I almost got rid of the gas pumps," he said. "I can't compete with the convenience stores on price. But then I saw how much the public appreciated it so I went with the feeling that it was the right thing to do. Luckily, it was."

So people drive over the rubber hose and it goes "ding" and Hensley comes out and asks the once-standard phrase, "Fill 'er up?" And while the gas is pumped into the vehicle, he lifts the hood, withdraws the oil stick, examines it, shows it to the driver, checks the tires, and washes the windshields, all at no extra cost.

It is the way nature intended things to be.

The station is at 924 North Main Street. To make an appointment with the past, call (928) 639–0432.

ONE FINE WATERING HOLE
Cleator

There is a Dogpatchian quality to this wide spot in the road. The houses, what few there are, have been touched by neither paintbrush nor stucco, so they're colored a weather-beaten brown and they spend their remaining days clinging to the side hills in mute desperation. A single dirt road meanders down into the valley, widens slightly in front of the Cleator Bar, and then trudges a weary path into the hills beyond.

The bar is open on only Fridays, Saturdays, and Sundays and, since it's the only place to go in Cleator, it is the hub of the community, if a town with only seven residents can be called either a community or a town. And since he owns the bar, permanent-resident Big Dave Rhodes is the social leader of Cleator, because he adjusts the bar schedule.

The bar is a wondrous place, a collection depot for nostalgia, a storehouse for memories, and a gathering place for tall tales. The floor is concrete. This sets the tone for the decor, which is American eclectic, a mix of early mining camp, cowboy bunkhouse, and junkyard, accented with used ball caps and old beer signs.

The clientele consists primarily of cowhands from nearby ranches and prospectors who come down from the surrounding hills. Their numbers are few, but that's okay because the bar holds only about twenty-five patrons.

The hours are "oh, from about noon to whenever on Fridays

and Saturdays," Rhodes said. "Whenever is usually a little while after it gets dark." The Sunday schedule is 10:00 A.M. to 4:00 P.M. unless nobody shows up. And on weekdays, if Big Dave's truck is there and you're really thirsty, it's okay to stop by and empty a glass of the house specialty, Big Dave's Pale Ale.

Cleator isn't hard to find but look quick or you'll miss it completely. It's about 14 miles west of Interstate 17 at exit 259. The bar's easy to spot because they painted it white. Once. A long time ago.

THE KEEPERS OF THE CROAKER
Congress

A n old frog squats along Highway 89 about half a mile north of downtown. Although exposed to the Arizona sun almost every day, the creature looks good, perhaps even better than it did when it was born, so to speak, more than three-quarters of a century ago.

But certain features set this amphibian apart. For example, it weighs an estimated 60 tons, stands 16 feet high, and is made of solid rock. And it needs a face-lift every now and then. The frog, a Congress landmark, existed in its natural state from prehistoric times until 1928, when it underwent a wondrous metamorphosis from rock to art.

Originally it was just a huge boulder perched on a hillside. Then Sara Perkins, a homesteader's wife, observed that if she squinted her eyes just right, the rock resembled a giant frog. So she and her sons painted it green on top, white on the bottom, gave it eyes and spots, and turned it into a tourist attraction. The Perkins family maintained the frog for years and when they left the area, the citizens of Congress became the unofficial keepers of the croaker.

The Congress Frog has withstood the elements for almost eighty years and gets a new coat of paint every time it needs one.

Now it gets a fresh paint job whenever the green fades because, as longtime-resident George Carter put it, "there ain't much else around here to look at so that frog is important to us."

THE BULLET UNDODGED

*A*uthor *Rose Mary Goodson gleaned this case of really rotten luck from old newspapers for her book,* The Story of Congress.

"Bad luck for a man named Thomas Concannon, a Lower Town Congress resident. He was mistaken for another and was seriously stabbed by a man. He recovered. A short time later, a woman named Mamie tried to shoot a gal named Sadie but missed. The bullet went wild and hit Concannon, killing him."

ART IN THE WILD
Cornville

Selecting the right adjectives to describe Eliphante can be difficult because there are so many capable of doing the job. Words like "interesting," "different," "unusual," "unique," "serene," "whimsical," and even that granddaddy of descriptive phrases for uncommon things, "far out."

Eliphante is an art complex on the banks of Oak Creek, and the art is unconventional. Michael Kahn, an oil painter, and weaver Leda Livant are responsible for the description-resistant place. They named it Eliphante when a friend observed that one of their odd-shaped (by normal standards) buildings looks like an elephant. And the structure that serves as their living quarters is called the Hippodome because it resembles a hippopotamus.

The centerpiece of the complex is Pipedreams, an art gallery built to display their work. It does not resemble any other art gallery anywhere. The exterior is dominated by a sculpture made of plastic pipe twisted into a form that looks like a giant kitchen whisk having a bad hair day. A door made of driftwood opens into a labyrinth of alcoves where the visitor is plunged into a surreal world of huge oil paintings, fabric ceilings, tile sculptures, and painted floors.

The grounds, covered with Astroturf, continue the theme with driftwood sculptures, a piece made of tractor wheels, and another composed of used volleyballs. "Sometimes, we just pick up something and it works," Livant said. So they have incorporated plywood, plastic netting, reflective foil, and broken ceramic tiles into their project because, as Kahn put it, "All life is art and Eliphante is our canvas."

The complex is open to the public but hard to reach, particularly when there's water in Oak Creek. Call (928) 634–4341 first and ask for directions.

AMMO ARCHITECTURE
Cottonwood

The Art Institute of Glitter Incorporated provides a good reason to bring up the old subject of beating your swords into plowshares.

The company creates and sells glitter, that sparkly stuff used in art, printing, clothing, interior design, and cosmetics.

Owner Barbara Trombley said the institute packages and ships more than 300 colors to buyers around the world.

But the building housing the enterprise has an ominous background. It is constructed of old ammunition boxes that once held shells for cannons. The empty boxes were stacked on top of each other to a height of 10 feet to form the walls and then secured with pieces of 1-by-6 lumber, so there are no studs. Once the stacks of empty ammo boxes reached the proper height, the roof trusses were put in place directly on top of them.

The ammo boxes were once common in the area and were frequently used as building material. They came from an army camp established near Flagstaff during World War II. Since the building has been covered with stucco, the boxes aren't visible. But Trombley keeps several of them out back to show the curious.

The institute is at 720 North Balboa in Cottonwood's Old Town.

A JOB FOR SIR LANCELOT
Dolan Springs

There's a dragon in Susan Pojmanski's front yard and it breathes fire.

This may not seem unusual to the locals, however. In the watering hole just down the street from her place, all six customers said they had seen unidentified flying objects and flying saucers. Most of them had more than one sighting to recount. One patron gave a detailed description of the superstructure of the craft he'd spotted. Another sipped on a draft beer and opined that it's because Dolan Springs is close to Area 51, a shadowy place in Nevada where the federal government allegedly keeps all sorts of secret stuff.

Susan Pojmanski's pet dragon breathes fire and attracts customers to her store in Dolan Springs.

Meanwhile, back at Star Country, the convenience market/gift shop owned and operated by Pojmanski and her husband, Jim, the dragon waited patiently for its next fire-breathing assignment. The creature, crafted from concrete by local artist Robert Long, burps fire and smoke only on special occasions, such as Halloween. And it's not caused by indigestion, as was the case back in medieval times. A propane tank connected to its innards fires this one. Long also created concrete flowers and a cement steer skull for the shop.

The fire breather and store are located at 15916 Pierce Ferry Road in Dolan Springs, which is about 31 miles north and 5 miles east of Kingman off U.S. 93. Dragon slayers and wannabe knights can find more information at starctry@ctaz.com or by calling (928) 767–4774.

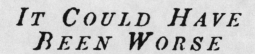

IT COULD HAVE BEEN WORSE

A nybody who has ever asked a child for some input can understand how Dead Horse Ranch State Park got its name.

It happened in the 1940s. The Ireys family migrated to Arizona from Minnesota and was looking for ranch land. At one of the sites they inspected, they came across a dead horse lying by the road. They passed on that property but then, after looking at several others, the parents asked the children which site they preferred.

Being children, they naturally chose "the one with the dead horse on it." The family not only bought the property, they also called it the Dead Horse Ranch. When the Arizona State Parks system purchased the site in 1973, the Ireys stipulated that the name be retained as one of the conditions of the sale.

It could have been worse. They might have found a dead musk ox or a deceased yak.

The park is on the Verde River on North Tenth Street in Cottonwood. For more information, call (928) 634–5283.

A NEW MINING METHOD
Goldroad

The Gold Road Mine began making money as long ago as 1902, when the original owners sold it for $50,000 before they had even mined an ounce of gold. By the end of 1907, the property had reportedly milled $2.25 million worth of the precious metal.

But because gold mining is such a fickle profession, the history of the mine since then has been off and on at best. It was almost abandoned after World War II, then it underwent a multimillion-dollar redevelopment shortly before the turn of this century and was fully operational from 1996 through 1998, employing 135 miners and producing 40,000 ounces of gold a year. It closed again in late 1998 when the price of gold fell below $300 an ounce.

Production could begin again when gold prices rise, and the owners say there's enough gold left in the hills to run for another ten years.

In the meantime the mine remains open on a limited basis. A staff of five or six conducts daily tours into the bowels of the earth, at one point taking their charges 300 feet below fabled Route 66. "So now," the guides declare, "we're mining the tourists for gold. And it's a lot easier."

The mine is located a couple of miles north of Oatman. Tours are offered daily. For information call (928) 768–1600 or visit www.goldroadmine.com.

QUINTESSENTIAL ROUTE 66
Hackberry

Picking a favorite nostalgia outlet along Route 66 can be difficult because Route 66 memorabilia is a big industry. But those who aren't interested in the complete story or those who merely want a sense of why the old highway receives so much attention can have their whims and curiosity satisfied by stopping at the Hackberry General Store, a place where time doesn't really pass; it just slowly meanders down the road.

Old cars and older cars share space with ancient gas pumps and other antiques at the Hackberry Store and Route 66 Museum.

The store is an old tin-roofed building that sits forlornly on a wide spot along Route 66. John and Kerry Pritchard bought it in 1998 and have filled it with castoffs, throwaways, and antiques. There's a soda fountain inside and hand-lettered signs ask visitors to help decide which chili is best. Souvenirs and snack-food displays share space with Marilyn Monroe photos and highway signs.

Outside, long-abandoned gas pumps stand silent guard duty across the storefront, and a Chevy Corvette like the one used in the *Route 66* television series waits for its next photo opportunity. And the building itself seems to be held together by old license plates and weathered tin signs.

The store is the only business in Hackberry, so it also serves as the Hackberry Visitor Center, even though there are no other tourist attractions in Hackberry either.

It's located on Route 66 about 24 miles east of Kingman. Those worried about not getting there in time to sample the chili should call (928) 769–2605 to see if they take reservations.

A MINE OF THEIR OWN
What Used to Be Haynes

The toughest part of rebuilding a ghost town is the aging process. Don Robertson knew that when he acquired one in 1980, so his first steps included buying an old sawmill and moving it onto the site. Then he started cutting pine logs into rough-sawn boards that he used to construct new buildings that look like old buildings.

His town was once called Haynes. It was a mining camp that went belly-up at a time when other mines in the area were yielding millions of dollars worth of copper. Robertson and his late wife, Terry, bought the remains with the intention of turning it into a mining museum. But they altered course and created the Gold King Mine, where tourists can lay their money down and get a taste of the alleged "good old days."

Only a couple of buildings from the original camp were still intact when the Robertsons arrived. The couple built new ones, then surrounded them with antique autos, mining equipment, and an old power generator that backfires so loudly that, Robertson claims, it'll produce rain if there are clouds in the area.

The mine is located in the hills just west of Jerome. Look for the sign near the fire station in Jerome. Nostalgia seekers may call (928) 634–0053 for directions and hours.

It Sure Looks Like a Numbskull
Hillside

Skulls, by their very nature, are usually hidden away where they're hard to find. The Giant Skull of Date Creek Road is somewhat of an exception. It's right out in the open, and it's been in the exact same spot for more than one hundred years, according to local legend.

The skull is actually a giant boulder painted white with black eyes and a black-rimmed mouth, so it looks a lot like a real skull even to those who are imaginationally challenged. Like many other pieces of rock art, the origins are hard to trace. But a newspaper clipping in a scrapbook at the Yarnell Public Library sheds some light.

In the story, published in the 1960s, former Santa Fe Railroad engineer Lee R. Roberts said he used to work the passenger trains that passed by the skull. He told the reporters he would conjure up wild tales about finding skulls in the area

*Because of its remote location, this huge rock skull frightens
rattlers and other critters but not train passengers.*

and then take delight in watching the passengers as the train
rounded a bend and the huge skull popped into view.

Roberts said a Santa Fe Railroad work crew painted the big
rock around 1900. They were in charge of painting the mile-
posts and other signs along the tracks and apparently had
paint and time left over when they finished their assigned
tasks. Passenger train service is a thing of the past in the area,
but the oversized cranium still sits next to the tracks.

Anatomy students and fans of poor Yorick can view the
remains by taking Yavapai County Road 62, also known as
Date Creek Road, for 6.3 miles west off Highway 89 just north
of Congress.

H IGH-C LASS J UNQUE
Humboldt

I magine, if you will, a place where everything you ever threw away one day then needed the next day has been gathered together and now lives in peace and harmony. Or imagine a place where all the treasures your mother tossed out when she cleaned your room after you left for college have been found, and now they're all waiting for you to touch each one and say you remember it.

There are such places. They exist, not only in the twilight zones or the back roads of the mind, but on the byways of reality. One of them is the Old Cracker Barrel Store, a last resort for those desperately in need of a 1947 desk calendar or a pillar from a Butterfield Stage Coach Line depot.

The sign says it's an antiques store, but it looks more like a place where discards go to die. When John and Betty Keeler started the business in the mid-1960s, they bought six vacant lots, erected a small building, and started acquiring inventory. Then things got out of hand. They got so much stuff they started buying old buildings to keep it in, and if they couldn't purchase the entire building, they took what they could.

All have been integrated into a grand scheme of clutter, a little village dedicated to the collection and dispersion of "previous user-enhanced collectibles." Or, as the Keelers prefer to call it, "junque." Their collection fills several buildings, the sidewalk, and a large area out back where there is no organization, only pathways through a realm of chaos. Artifacts even spill into the front yard of their nearby home, where the walks are lined with petunias growing in toilet bowls.

Due to the tremendous pressures involved in keeping their stock current, the Keelers open their store only Sundays through Thursdays. For more information, call (928) 632-9455.

BROTHER, CAN YOU SPARE A PENNY?
Jerome

A long time ago copper was the reason this town prospered. The mines here began operating around 1876, but Native Americans had been taking the ore from the ground for centuries before that. The copper boom produced a community of 15,000, but the good times didn't last. By the 1950s, Jerome was a shadow of its former self, inhabited by a few diehards and a handful of counterculturists.

Now it's making a comeback. The population is still around only 500, but the town has become a tourist mecca. Folks by the thousands drive up Mingus Mountain to visit the shops, galleries, and eateries that have taken over the old buildings once occupied by mining firms.

And copper is making another contribution, although not as substantial as the first time around. This time it's pennies, not ore. Pennies and an outhouse. On Jerome's main thoroughfare, in a large hole in the ground that used to be a basement, there sits one of those basic wooden structures once fondly referred to as a "two-holer," and it's surrounded by signs urging visitors to throw their money down the toilet.

A lot of them do. Every day, tourists by the hundreds pitch coins toward the outhouse, trying to make one plop into one of the holes. It's not easy. The little house is surrounded by wrought-iron fencing so the coin throwers can't get close. This eliminates cheap slam-dunking. And retrieving your missed shots.

That doesn't deter the flippers and tossers. Their penchant for this type of hole-in-one shooting nets about $1,000 a month for the Jerome Historical Society, the people in charge of collecting the daily offerings.

Feel like giving your Lincoln a toss? The outhouse awaits your pennies on Main Street, right down the block from the Jerome Historical Society Mine Museum.

GETTING A BANG OUT OF CHURCH
Jerome

The Powderbox Church is now a private residence that sits on one of Jerome's many hills, sheltered by several large cypress trees. But its origins involve such nonreligious elements as racism and dynamite.

The structure was erected in 1939 by Mexican miners who were banned from the all-white Methodist church and needed a place to worship. Since building materials were both expensive and scarce, the miners used empty dynamite boxes to construct the shell. There were ample dynamite boxes available because the explosive was used frequently in the mining process.

Ironically, once the church was completed, the white Methodists invited the Mexicans into their congregation.

The building is occasionally opened to the public during Jerome's annual Home and Historic Building Tours. It sits on a hillside on the south side of the road leading to Jerome State Park. But there's a better view from up above, on the main road leading into the business district. For more information, call (928) 634–1066.

A RECYCLED RECYCLER
Kingman

The Powerhouse Visitor Center here is a classic example of how to recycle a recycling plant. It's also a great place to find out what it feels like to stand exactly 3333.33 feet above sea level.

The center is housed in an old structure originally built in 1907 as a powerhouse to produce electricity for nearby mining operations. But the completion of Hoover Dam in 1938 brought about cheap hydroelectric power and spelled the end of the Kingman generating facility. It stopped producing in 1940 and was abandoned in 1970.

As buildings with 18-inch-thick concrete walls are so often inclined to do, the powerhouse just sat there and deteriorated because nobody could afford to knock it down. Then the Powerhouse Gang organized a campaign to rehabilitate it. After acquiring the property they had to lease it to a recycling company to create a cash flow. That agreement ended in 1993 and the restoration process began.

Now the building houses the Kingman Area Chamber of Commerce and its Tourist Information Center, as well as a Route 66 Museum, a photography gallery, gift shop, sandwich shop, and model railroad store. A model train makes regular runs through the spacious center every day and a sign at the front door says those who enter are doing so at precisely 3333.33 feet above sea level.

The designers incorporated the old concrete walls into the architecture of the building, and they cleverly installed a cellphone tower and then camouflaged it as a smoke stack.

The center is located at 120 West Andy Devine Avenue. Thick-wall enthusiasts can call (928) 753–6106 for directions.

REQUIEM FOR A HEAVYWEIGHT
Kingman

S ome cowboy-movie stars achieved fame for their ability to ride horses, whip bad guys, or sing a song. Andy Devine was not particularly skilled in any of those categories. But he's

*Actor Andy Devine, now honored in a museum in Kingman, was big
in both real life and reel life.*

a native son here, and such a hero to the people of Kingman
that they have named a street after him and dedicated a major
portion of a local museum to his memory.

Devine was best known for his raspy voice (the result of a
childhood accident that damaged his larynx), his size (he once
weighed in at 358 pounds), and his role as Jingles P. Jones,
saddle pal of Wild Bill Hickok, portrayed by Guy Madison in
the movies and on television.

After brief careers as a professional football player, life-
guard, telephone lineman, and news photographer, he broke
into show business as a regular on *The Jack Benny Show*.
Devine would eventually appear in more than 400 movies, but
always as a sidekick, never as a leading man.

A major thoroughfare was renamed Andy Devine Avenue in 1955, and the Kingman Area Chamber of Commerce presents Andy Awards every year to outstanding citizens. Before his death in 1977, the actor returned to his hometown many times to participate in the annual Andy Devine Days. And the new Mohave Museum of History and Arts contains a large Andy Devine exhibit that features old photos, movie posters, and clippings.

The museum is at 400 West Beale Street, just a block off Andy Devine Avenue. For information, call (928) 753–3195.

A BRIDGE OVER THE SAND
Lake Havasu City

D espite what the nursery rhyme says, the London Bridge didn't fall down. It was dismantled and moved to Arizona.

The history of the London Bridge dates from A.D. 43 when the Romans built a pontoon bridge across the River Thames. The first permanent bridge was constructed a short time later and apparently lasted until 1014, when the Vikings pulled it down. The first stone bridge was built in 1176 and stood until 1824, when a new one was erected. That's the one that now sits in the Mohave Desert at Lake Havasu City.

The bridge was put up for sale by the city of London because it was slowly sinking into the river. Robert P. McCulloch, the entrepreneur who founded Lake Havasu City in 1964, paid $2,460,000 for it because he figured it would help land sales in his proposed city. Every stone was numbered before the bridge was taken apart and shipped across the Atlantic, through the Panama Canal, and up the Pacific to Long Beach, California, where the huge granite blocks were loaded onto trucks and hauled to this Colorado River site.

Once in Lake Havasu City, the bridge was reconstructed over a barren stretch of sand. When the rebuilding was complete, the sand was removed and a channel was cut, allowing Colorado River water to flow under the bridge. The total cost of the project was an estimated $7.5 million.

It was, in the estimation of one English visitor to the scene, such an American way of doing things.

SALVAGING THE SEPTICS
Lake Havasu City

The Creative Cultural Center is a place where old septic tanks go to get makeovers.

The center is a homegrown community attraction that promotes area culture and heritage through the sale of local artwork, stage presentations by a group of re-enactors, and tours of the Colorado River.

It is also a minirecycling plant; everything in the facility was built with donated and recycled materials and nothing goes to waste. Rocks from the construction process now form a huge turtle, snake, and lizard montage outside the front entrance. Leftover concrete irrigation pipes were used as pillars to support a ramada covered with donated palm fronds. The front sides of decommissioned refrigerators provide storage space for clay and pottery; the backs have been stuccoed to look like an old brick wall.

Out in the garden the center found a use for several septic tanks that were deemed unworthy of their original purpose. They were hauled onto the lot and converted into minigardens. Each tank has been filled with soil, then painted and decorated with symbols, slogans, and other art forms by the gardeners. Rows of corn, beans, melons, peas, and flowers sprout from the tanks. Good thing that they're all at waist level so the tillers of the soil don't have to risk underwear exposure, those embarrassing rips caused by bending over to pull out a weed. Horticulturists interested in septic-tank farming can visit the center at 1350 McCulloch Boulevard, or call (928) 855–7300.

A Symbol for Number One
Mayer

If anything really big ever happens here, something that's so big the community can lay claim to being Number One in that particular category, there's a great symbol already in place. It's a 125-foot smokestack that never got a chance.

The smokestack, on a hill along Highway 69 as it divides Mayer, was erected in 1917 by the Great Western Smelter Company. But the smelter closed before the stack was put into operation. Today it's the sole reminder of an industry that produced millions in copper, zinc, and lead.

A Prescott businessman once bought the smokestack. He thought it was made of brick, so he planned to knock it down and use the bricks to build a house. But it's poured concrete. "Let me tell you, that was a big surprise," he said.

There's also a story about the smokestack and the Alpine chambermaid, a young woman from Switzerland who once worked at a Mayer hotel. While hanging out at a local watering hole, a bunch of miners bet some cowboys that she could climb the stack. Both sides were placing $100 bets. The miners won when she climbed to the top. There's no record of whether the miners gave her a tip.

Now the smokestack just stands there like a big Number One, patiently waiting for somebody to do something worthy of Number Oneness so it can be a symbol.

THE ANSWER TO "WHATCHA DOIN'?"
Nothing

Nothing appears on the map as a little red square, but calling it a town or even a hamlet is an exaggeration. There's something at Nothing, but it's not much more than nothing. The entire complex consists of two buildings plus the trailer house where Buddy Kenworthy and his family live, and an old school bus that is occasionally occupied when they get company. Buddy owns Nothing and everything in it, which, as the name indicates, isn't much.

Buddy Kenworthy (right) built Nothing so people would know what Nothing looks like. His assistant in the endeavor is Jim Hay (left), also known as Old Miner Jim.

Basically it's a wide spot in the road where travelers can buy snacks and soft drinks or, in case of emergency, get towed. One handpainted sign lists the population as four; another gives the Nothing motto: THE STAUNCH CITIZENS OF NOTHING ARE FULL OF FAITH, HOPE AND BELIEVE IN THE WORK ETHIC. THROUGH THE YEARS, THESE DEDICATED PEOPLE HAD FAITH IN NOTHING, HOPED FOR NOTHING, WORKED AT NOTHING, ALL FOR NOTHING.

Near the store entrance, a sign atop a small basket warns BEWARE OF THE COPPERHEADS. The basket contains several nonpoisonous pennies. Inside, the walls and ceilings are covered with notes left by Playboy bunnies, Frank Zappa, foreign visitors, and everyday passersby. "I stopped at Nothing and bought something," one says. Another reads, "Nothing is really something."

The original Nothing was a couple of miles down the road. It was destroyed by fire in 1988, so Kenworthy moved his operation closer to the highway. This makes it easier for people to find Nothing.

Those interested in seeing what Nothing looks like will stumble across it on Highway 93 about 40 miles north of Wickenburg.

THE ANSWER TO "WHERE YOU BEEN?"
Nowhere

Yes, Carolina, there is a Nowhere. It lies in the high desert and it soothes the agony of those who traverse a winding stretch of road that goes up the mountain to Prescott. As one might expect, there's a whole lot of nothing in Nowhere, because there's nothing there except an old saloon and a trailer court.

But there's usually somebody in the saloon willing to debate the eternal questions of whether there actually is such a place as Nowhere and, equally important, whether the name should be spelled Nowhere or No Where. Opinion is a unanimous "yup" on the first, and nobody really cares much about the second, as long as the beer holds out.

The saloon is officially the Burro Inn. There are neither burros nor sleeping facilities on the premises, although some patrons have been known to spend the night in deep repose atop the pool table. Parts of the building have been around since 1851 when it served as a way station for stage lines. It has been remodeled, reconstructed, and renovated several times since, and even the regulars have some difficulty telling the old from the new.

The property became Nowhere several years ago when then-owner Marion Wade bought it with high hopes of establishing a place where being nobody was a matter of importance. She planned to incorporate the area as a town called Nowhere and open a post office so she could get franking privileges. Neither happened, but the name stuck. Current owner Darrel Hardy has left the place pretty much as he found it.

Those who want to get to Nowhere fast will find it on Highway 89 next to Wilhoit, which is between Yarnell and Prescott. If you miss it, call (928) 442–3287.

B U R R O S   A N D   B I S C U I T S
O a t m a n

The unofficial census rolls for Oatman contain 12 to 14 burros and about 150 humans. The burros are listed first because they provide much of the economic base for the humans.

The animals are descendants of the working burros that were turned loose in the desert by miners more than a century ago. They come down from the surrounding hills every day and take up their posts along Oatman's main drag. There they

*Burros are a major economic force in Oatman, so they
can go where they please.*

consort with the tourists, many of whom come here specifically
to go one-on-one with a burro. And the tourists feed the burros,
take their pictures, and buy burro post cards.

Most merchants, therefore, offer burro-related items, such as
burro feed, burro figurines made of papier mâché and goat
hair, burro T-shirts, burro bumper stickers, and burro calendars. The bumper stickers and calendars are big sellers.
Because the burro is also known as an ass, those items substitute "ass" for "burro" any time they can, as in "hauling burro"
and "kicking some burro."

The animals have the run of the city during their daily for-
ays, and motorists are cautioned that hitting a burro will
result in a major fine. During the foaling season the person

who first spots a newborn posts a notice on the bulletin board at the post office, and the town gives it a name.

And, of course, the burros also provide the essential tools vital to the annual Burro Biscuit Toss. Prior to the event volunteers go into the desert to select used burro deposits. Desert droppings are preferred to those left on Main Street because they're harder and hold their shape better when propelled. The biscuits are then painted gold, and contestants pick their favorites and toss them down the street in front of crowds of cheering spectators. The biscuit that sails the farthest is declared the winner. The winning tosser gets cash and merchandise prizes as well as a fresh bar of soap.

The event is held during Gold Camp Days over the Labor Day weekend. Biscuiteers needing more information should call (928) 768-7400.

SOLAR EGG FRYING
Oatman

Nobody looks at the thermometer in Oatman during the summer. The first person on the street every day looks up and says, "Hot." Then everybody else says, "Yup," and that takes care of the weather report.

But the summer heat, intense as it is, also gives the community a reason to hold one of its major events every Fourth of July. It's the Oatman Sidewalk Egg Fry, which has been going on since the 1970s.

The name is a bit misleading. The sidewalks in Oatman are mostly wood, so they don't conduct heat as well as cement or asphalt. This does not deter the Oatman citizenry, however. They merely adjusted the rules to allow any egg fried by the sun as a legitimate contender. So contestants fry their eggs with solar panels, mirrors, foil, and magnifying glasses.

They get fifteen minutes to make an egg edible. That in itself is a challenge because the judges are selected from the viewing audience and, not being professional egg-frying adjudicators, often balk at eating a half-fried egg. But once again the rules were relaxed. "We tell the judges to just pick the one they think looks like it's fried the best," said Jackie Rowland, who runs a gift shop called Fast Fanny's Place and directs the chamber of commerce.

About thirty teams enter the contest every year. For details, call Rowland at (928) 768-7400.

GERTIE'S OWN FIRE DEPARTMENT
Peach Springs

Gertie is a replication of a mummified sloth discovered in a cave almost a century ago. She is a primary attraction at Grand Canyon Caverns and justifiably so, since she is the only one of her kind displayed in Arizona.

But Gertie's old and getting older, and her popularity is being challenged by something a bit more up-to-date and infinitely more colorful—a ride in a fire engine. The owners of the caverns have purchased two vintage red units and are the only people in the state to offer daily fire-truck rides. But the faux firemen ride only on the surface; the paths in the caverns are much too steep to allow underground antics. A ride costs $8.00, but it's only $5.00 with a paid admission to the caverns.

The limestone caverns, although not quite as exciting as roaring around with the sirens blaring, are twenty-one stories below the surface. Gertie is strategically placed along the pathway. She represents "glossotherium harlani," a creature that stood about 16 feet tall, weighed up to 1,200 pounds, and became extinct about 20,000 years ago. Her closest living relatives are tree sloths and armadillos.

The Grand Canyon Caverns are on Route 66 about 65 miles east of Kingman. For information call (928) 422–3223. But they don't let Gertie answer the phone.

GREAT CAESAR'S GHOST

*T*his has the makings of a good story:

An old church scheduled for demolition is saved from the wrecking ball by a group of dedicated citizens who convert it into a fine-arts center. But then they discover the ghost.

It's nothing official, such as the Phantom of the Opera or those squishy things in Ghostbusters, but there are rumors that a ghost does indeed live in the old church that now houses the Prescott Fine Arts Association gallery and theater.

Since ghosts don't hand out business cards or write their autobiographies, this one is a little hard to track. But the rumors say it's the spirit of Father Edmund Clossen, an itinerant Catholic priest who worked among area Indian tribes and often stayed in the church. After his death in 1902, his body was buried under the altar. His remains were relocated to a local cemetery in 1906.

And now when actors are getting into costume in the dressing area, they say they hear the priest's ghost rattling a door upstairs. One director claimed he saw a shadow crossing in front of a painted set. Another director said that after a production of Blithe Spirit, he and three actors saw drinking glasses rise from the stage and drop to the floor.

But at least the ghost doesn't crinkle cellophane wrappers or talk on a cell phone during the show.

The theater is at 208 North Marina in downtown Prescott.

A MUSEUM BUILT BY IMPOSTERS
Prescott

The Smoki Museum of American Indian Art and Culture is recognized as an important keeper of Native American artifacts due to its excellent collection of authentic items from several Indian cultures.

It's a bit ironic, because the Smoki People who founded the museum were white folks pretending to be Indians, and the name they selected for their group wasn't even close to an Indian name.

This curious alliance began in 1921 when the Prescott Frontier Days Rodeo needed something to boost attendance. Local businessmen came up with the idea of a snake dance using live snakes. They shaved their bodies, dressed up in fancy costumes, and put on a sort of burlesque show. But they were such an unexpected success they began taking themselves seriously and broke away from the rodeo.

Over the next six decades, they researched Indian ceremonial dances and presented them to sellout crowds. But by the 1980s, criticism of their shows by both Anglos and Indians increased and interest in their organization waned, so the group disbanded. Now the old-timers hold annual meetings and wonder which one will eventually be known as the Last of the Smokis.

The museum the federal government and the Smokis built in 1933 to display their personal artifacts is still going. It's tucked behind a large armory at 147 North Arizona Street, and it's open daily from April 15 through September 30. Smoki fans and even non-Smokiers can get information by calling (928) 445–1230.

THEIR STATION IN LIFE
Prescott

Purkeypile's Shell Station is a classic off-the-beaten-path spot. Although it's within the city limits, it's down at the end of a dirt road, tucked away in the pines. This place is so isolated that if you don't know exactly where it is, you probably won't find it.

But those who do stumble across it, either by accident or with explicit directions, will discover one of life's little pleasantries. It's actually the family garage, but it has been converted into an old-fashioned service station and restaurant where gasoline costs 19 cents a gallon, a hamburger goes for 20 cents, and an O Henry candy bar is still a nickel.

None of this is for real, of course. It's sort of an adult playhouse, created and maintained by Don and Lil Purkeypile because, in their own words, "It's something we always wanted to do."

They started the project in 1992, after moving to Prescott from Reno. But they had been collecting stuff for almost twenty-five years before that. Now a lot of that stuff is on display in an authentic setting. It includes gas pumps from the early 1900s, a phone booth, a revolving barber pole, a soft-drink cooler, a malted-milk maker, and rows of oilcans. Plus an assortment of old cars and trucks, Burma Shave signs, a traffic signal, old license plates from every state along Route 66, and steel signs with thermometers.

The couple has divided the garage into three sections. One houses Lil's Cafe, where the menu board lists 5-cent Kool Aid, black-and-white-checkered linoleum covers the floor, and 1940s music still plays on the jukebox. The second part is the working garage, complete with the smell of old crankcase oil and filled with hood ornaments, fan belts, a barber chair, and old radios in wooden cases. And the third sector is the fix-up area where Don works to restore his old cars. They all function properly, and viewing them is free. If you can get there.

The address is 2016 Acorn Drive. But call (928) 445–2048 before trying to find it by yourself. They'll give you directions. Have a writing tool and a big piece of paper handy.

MINING THE HARD WAY

*O*ne of the first things a miner should learn is to be careful where he puts his pick. As proof, consider an item from the May 13, 1899, edition of the Prescott Journal Miner concerning one J. M. Moore and how he discovered the Amulet Mine.

According to the report, Moore was prospecting on Lynx Creek when the heat and humidity got to him so he took a brief rest. "Upon rising to resume his trip," the story said, "he threw the pick on his shoulder. In doing so he struck his back, causing himself severe pain. Taking the pick from his shoulder, he stuck it into the ground, accompanied by an exclamation that it could stay there.

"On reconsideration he pulled the pick out of the ground and found to his surprise that it had penetrated into rich material. He began prospecting and found fabulously rich silver ore . . . ."

WILL THIS THING FLY?
Prescott

The acquisition of spaceships is difficult; they're never listed under SPACESHIPS FOR SALE in the want ads. Steve LaVigne found one, however. It doesn't have warp drive, and the photon torpedoes have been disarmed. But the price was right. LaVigne and a friend bought it for $100 in 1984. They also had to remove the craft from its landing site as part of the transaction.

This may be the only spaceship in the world powered by a super-duper phistifized zoozer with Mach-1 power. At least, it's the only one of its kind in Prescott.

Since then LaVigne has become the sole owner of the ship and has uncovered much of its history. His research indicates the space vehicle was created as a prop for *Tobor the Great,* a 1954 sci-fi movie starring Charles Drake and Karen Booth. Although allegedly a spaceship, it was built on a semitrailer and has wheels. Somehow the thing either flew or drove to the Prescott area, where it became part of Walsh's Mountain Fantasy, an amusement park owned by Rodney Walsh. When the park closed, Walsh donated the alien craft to the city of Prescott. Unable to find a suitable pilot, the city gave it to a local rehabilitation facility.

After buying it from the rehab center, the new owners came across some construction workers who were willing to move it for free if they could drive it up and down Prescott's Whiskey Row, an infamous blocklong assortment of spirits dispensaries and saloons. The space vehicle was then taken to LaVigne's property.

It's still there, sitting amid a row of old buses behind the local Coca-Cola distributorship along Highway 69 on the southeastern edge of Prescott.

A MAN'S HOME IS HIS CASTLE
Prescott Valley

E ven before Ken Server bought his retirement home in Prescott Valley, he noticed that the slope of the lot dropped about 30 feet from back to front. But he liked the area and figured he could landscape his yard to reduce the incline. To accomplish that, he started collecting rocks.

That was in 1996. He used all the rocks he found and still looks for more. He located them in his own neighborhood, at construction sites, and along roadsides. He has no idea how many rocks he has collected but estimates it's in the tens of thousands. Nor does he know how much sand and concrete he used to stick all of them together.

But the end result is something to behold.

First, Server terraced his property. Then he built concrete-block retaining walls and covered them with rocks. Some of the rocks came from California, Nevada, and Tennessee, where he worked during his career as a mining engineer. He uses neither blueprint nor plan. "Each day, when I come out here, I have no idea where I'm headed," he said.

The rockscape winds around his house and includes arches and pillars and places that look like they were put there so archers could launch their arrows at advancing armies. "Sometimes people stop and ask if it's an old castle or an Indian ruin," Server said. Once he finishes installing rocks, he plans to build a waterfall that will cascade from level to level into a pool.

The home that is almost a castle is near the corner of Stageway and Sunflower in Prescott Valley. The man doing the stonework will be Ken Server.

VORTEXTURIZED
Sedona

One problem with a vortex is that many people don't know how to describe two or more of them. (Either "vortices" or "vortexes" is acceptable.) Another problem is that most people have their own idea of what a vortex actually is.

And in these parts that's a big point, because the vortex is a good source of income.

There are those, and they are many, who believe Sedona is a major center for unseen forces that go by such descriptions as "meditative sites," "electromagnetic force fields," "upflows," and "crystals." But even the believers are divided on the alleged power sources said to inhabit the towering red rocks that surround the community.

Some say they are the result of a powerful crystal buried by aliens under a huge sandstone formation called Bell Rock. Some say Bell Rock itself is an alien spacecraft. Others claim there are forces that make contemplation and meditation so intense they become spiritual experiences.

Regardless of who believes what, vortexes are big business here, spawning at least a dozen related enterprises. New Age stores and crystal shops sell a variety of items that reportedly enhance the vortex experience. Other operations offer guided tours of the best vortex spots, seminars on how to detect when you're most receptive to the power of the vortex, and instructions on how to find deeper dimensions related to vortices.

Believers and skeptics alike can get more information from the Sedona Visitors Center at (928) 282-7722

A FASHION STATEMENT IN TEAL GREEN
Sedona

Their golden arches readily identify the thousands of McDonald's fast-food eateries all over the world. But not in Sedona.

In Sedona the arches are teal green. They're the only ones in the world painted that color. It came about in the early 1990s when McDonald's wanted to put a restaurant in Sedona. But Sedona wanted something different to preserve its small-town feeling. "We asked if they'd be willing to change the color of the arches to teal green to match the signage already in place at the shopping center," said John O'Brien, director of community development for the city. "They didn't like it at first but

then acquiesced. After that, they were very easy to work with."
Now the restaurant itself markets the teal green arches as the
only ones of their kind anywhere in the world.

Some things remain unchanged, however. Ronald McDonald
still has red hair and Grimmis is still purple, even in Sedona.

The teal arches and the restaurant that accompanies them
are at 2380 West Highway 89A in Sedona.

IT COULD HAVE BEEN BEATS ME CANYON

M *any of the red-rock formations that surround
this city have earned their names by resem-
bling common items, such as a coffeepot, steamboat,
merry-go-round, and lizard head. But there's nothing in the official city history that explains Damfino
Canyon.*

*According to local legend, however, it happened
this way:*

*Back in the 1930s, while the Civilian Conserva-
tion Corps was mapping the area, an engineer asked
one of the workers the name of a particularly
treacherous canyon so he could mark it on his map.
Since the canyon had never been named, the worker
replied, "Damned if I know."*

*The engineer thought he said "Damfino," so
that's what he wrote down. The canyon still bears
the name.*

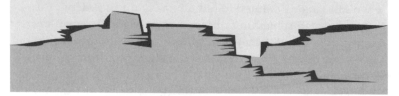

S AGAS OF THE O PEN R OAD
S e l i g m a n

The Snow Cap Café may be the only restaurant in the world where a request for ice cream evokes the question, "Do you want mustard on that?" And before the befuddled customer can reply, Juan Delgadillo delivers a squirt from a yellow plastic bottle. The squirted customer shrieks; everyone else laughs. The mustard is actually yellow string, the key prop in a standby gag at the Snow Cap.

Delgadillo used scrap lumber to build the tiny establishment in 1953 and still shows up for work every day, even though he observed his eighty-sixth birthday in 2002. The string-of-mustard trick is his favorite, but there are several others in his repertoire. Ask for a small Coke and it comes in a dinky paper ketchup container. Ask for ice and he brings out a quart of frozen shavings.

The interior is covered with business cards from around the world and signs advertising SLIGHTLY USED NAPKINS and DEAD CHICKEN SPECIALS. A 1936 Chevrolet truck adorned with a decorated Christmas tree stands outside the cafe and the backyard is a mélange of Route 66 memorabilia, his-and-her outhouses, and plastic artwork.

Just down the street, Angel Delgadillo, Juan's brother, talks about the bygone days of straight-razor shaves and dispenses folksy advice in the tiny barbershop he operated for decades. Although he was born in 1926, many consider Angel Delgadillo a superhero; he saved the town and the stretch of Route 66 that runs through it. Concerned that the town was dying after Interstate 40 bypassed it, Angel spearheaded a drive to organize the Historic Route 66 Association to promote the old

road as an alternative to the freeway. Now tour buses, motorcycle caravans, foreign tourists, and a wide variety of others
leave the four-lane hustle for a look at what used to be.

Seligman is about midway between Williams and Kingman.
For information on anything relative to the good old days, call
(928) 422–3352.

JUST FOLLOW THE ANTLERS
Seligman

Nothing is real hard to find in Seligman because Seligman is
not very big. Everything is "a couple blocks down that
way" or "a couple blocks down that other way."

But Tim Pender's place is extra easy to come by. It's the one
surrounded by the horny fence on the south side of Route 66.
The fence is actually chain-link, but it's covered with hundreds
of antlers, small and large, from deer and elk. Pender doesn't
know exactly how many he has, but there are enough to create
a 3-foot barrier around his house.

And in case some of the antlers begin showing wear and
tear, he has a small storage shed filled with replacements. Pender is a wildlife manager for the Arizona Game and Fish
Department. He is the sole manager for two units that cover a
total of 3,600 square miles, which is more than two million
square acres. This gives him a lot of area for antler hunting.
He elected to live in Seligman because the landscape is flat and
"when I look outside, I like to see a long way."

He finds most of the antlers after they've been shed by their
original owners. "I just like antlers," he said. "I can't walk by

Tim Pender gave his antler collection purpose by using it to
build a fence around his home in Seligman.

one. I have to pick it up. I guess you'd call me a sort of an addict."

The fence has become a tourist attraction. One day the family found a group of foreign sightseers roaming around in their living room, taking pictures of Pender's hunting trophies. "I guess they thought it was a museum," he chuckled.

WHERE TIME TAKES A REST
Skull Valley

The Skull Valley General Store performs its "Symphony of the Floor Boards" every day. Years ago all general stores had such melodies, generated by the hardwood floors squeaking under the footsteps of those who trod across them.

It was a discordant kind of music, the beat established by how fast the squeakist walked across the floor. The songs were mournful but comforting, because the general store was the hub of activity, a gathering place where friends met.

The creaky floors and the general stores are almost all gone now, replaced by in-and-out establishments where nobody knows anybody. But on the back roads, a few old-timers still play that haunting melody again and again to welcome both friend and stranger.

It's that way at the Skull Valley General Store, where owners Archy and Laurica McDonald sell basic necessities, ship packages, take phone messages, and provide a meeting place for their community. They greet customers by name, cash their checks, tell them how fresh the eggs are, and listen to their jokes.

"We're Information Central," Archy said. "We can see the whole downtown from here and everybody watches out for everybody else. There are only about 75 of us in town and maybe another 200 in the surrounding area. And, fortunately, it isn't growing."

The store was built in 1916 and retains much of its original flavor, including the squeaky floors and the sense of belonging.

Those who yearn to return will find the store on Iron Springs Road right across the street from the Skull Valley Service station. For directions, call (928) 442-3351.

DOING THE YABBA-DABBA THING
Valle

Fred Flintstone and Barney Rubble, or reasonable facsimiles thereof, greet visitors every day at Bedrock City, a combination amusement park, gift shop, and restaurant that has been occupying a big chunk of ground here for more than thirty years.

The Flintstone characters, immortalized in cartoons and movies for more than four decades, are only statues in the park, but they're authentic. Linda Speckels, the owner, has to stay current with licensing arrangements dictated by whatever corporation owns the Flintstone name.

Fred Flintstone and the skeleton of a vehicular dinosaur greet visitors at Bedrock City near the Grand Canyon.

The statues of Fred, Barney, Wilma, Pebbles, Bam-Bam, and the rest pose for photos. They then point the way to the theater where Flintstone cartoons run continuously, the ride through a miniature volcano on a toy train, and the Dino-Slide.

Linda's late husband, Hudi, was a government contractor when he built the park in 1972. The twenty-acre facility also encompasses a large parking lot, a campground, and Fred's Diner, where the menu includes Dino Dogs, Bronto Burgers, and Chickasaurus sandwiches.

Bedrock City is on the corner of State Route 64 and Highway 180. The phone number is (928) 635-2600. There's an admission charge, but it might be reduced if you can do a perfect "yabba dabba doo" without embarrassing your family.

MacArthur's Connie
Valle

Most people never have the opportunity to plop down on the same seat that once held the rear end of Gen. Douglas MacArthur, but the chance is real at the Planes of Fame Air Museum here. One of the planes on display is the huge Lockheed C-121A Constellation that once served as MacArthur's personal carrier during the Korean War.

The plane, officially named "Bataan" but nicknamed "Connie," was the general's transport for seventeen missions over Korea. Their last flight together took him to San Francisco after President Harry Truman fired him as supreme commander of the allied forces. The plane was also used during the Berlin airlift, then by NASA as part of the Apollo space program. It is one of 30 on display at the museum and one of more than 160 owned by Californian Ed Maloney, owner of the museum.

Of course there's a price to be paid for the honor of sitting where the general sat, and it's in addition to the $5.00 entry fee. Only those who pay an additional $3.00 get to tour the inside of the aircraft. Those who don't pay the extra charge don't have to go away unfulfilled, however. MacArthur's plane is so big it can't fit inside the museum, so it sits outside in plain view but surrounded by a fence.

The plane, the museum, and a huge eagle sculpture are near the corner of Highway 180 and State Route 64. They're available daily except Christmas and Thanksgiving. For more details, call (928) 635-1000.

GOLFING WITHOUT GREENS FEES
Wikieup

The pros will never stop for a tune-up round at the Coyote Canyon Golf Course. But golfers who don't earn millions on the tour will find it a bargain, because there are no greens fees. And sometimes, even the golf balls are complimentary.

The course is a nine-hole layout built by Forrest Purdy and his wife, Jan, because they love the game and wanted to share their enthusiasm with others. A notice on the driving range urges golfers to hurry if others are waiting to play. And a sign in the window of the mobile home that serves as a clubhouse says loose balls found on the driving range and ninth fairway may be used but must be left on the course after a round because they belong to the country club.

Equally important is the sign on the gate. It reads: COURSE OPEN. CATTLE ON COURSE. KEEP GATE CLOSED. And there are cattle grazing on the fairways, but they're kind and considerate. And they never laugh when you miss a 6-inch putt.

The course is located at the corner of Country Club Drive and Golf Course Avenue on the south side of Wikieup, just east of Highway 93 as it passes through town. There's no phone but that's okay—they don't reserve tee times.

THE MYSTERIOUS SNOOPY
Wikieup

On the north side of town, a white rocket ridden by three cartoon characters welcomes visitors to Wikieup. The rocket appears to be a sawed-off telephone pole painted white and outfitted with a red nose cone and tail fins. The astronauts are wood cutouts of Snoopy, his feathered friend Woodstock, and his brother Spike, all familiar to fans of the "Peanuts" comic strip.

Snoopy captains a rocket ship headed for nowhere, stranded on the main street of Wikieup.

But, although the contraption seems to serve as a friendly greeting to those who drive by, it doesn't appear to be held in much esteem by the locals, making tracing its origins almost impossible. Two women at the post office said it was erected by "a foreign couple," then explained that "foreign means they ain't from around here." A woman in a gift shop responded to inquiries with, "You don't want to know what I think of that thing. It's a disgrace but it's on private property so we can't get rid of it."

No Trespassing and Beware of Dog signs on the property discourage further research.

Apparently the rocket was built by a couple of winter visitors from Michigan in the early 1990s. They sold out and went back home, leaving Snoopy and his mates stranded on the launch pad.

The astronauts and spacecraft are on the west side of Highway 93, which also serves as Wikieup's main drag.

THE BROTHEL REBORN
Williams

From the very beginning the Red Garter has been a labor of love. The early occupants sold love and the early patrons bought it. And now John Holst takes care of it with loving hands.

The structure that houses the Red Garter Bed and Bakery was built in 1897 and served as a bordello for more than forty years. The girls plied their trade on the second floor, which was reachable only by a twenty-one-step staircase known as "the cowboys' endurance test." After the law clamped down on that form of diversion, the building became a flophouse, a restaurant, and a warehouse.

When Holst bought it in 1979, there were 4,000 old tires stacked up inside. He quit his regular job and worked full-time at converting the brothel into a bed-and-breakfast establishment with a bakery where the saloon used to be. Most traces of its former use are gone.

Except for Eve.

According to some guests, there's a ghostly woman in a long dress who wanders from room to room at night. Holst says he's never seen her, but he gets periodic reports of "something strange." One guest, he said, "made a strong connection and named her Eve, so that's what we call her. She's harmless and shy."

For those interested in sleeping over with Eve, the Red Garter is at 137 West Railroad Avenue. For further information, visit the Web site at www.redgarter.com, or call (800) 328-1484.

A SHRINE OF CONCRETE AND ROCKS
Yarnell

Nobody can say for sure that miracles have actually happened at the Shrine of St. Joseph of the Mountains. But on the other hand, nobody can say for sure that they haven't, either. This uncertainty does not bother the thousands of people who come here every year to pause, reflect and, perhaps, pray for miracles.

Just the existence of the shrine borders on the miraculous, considering the circumstances. It was built by a dishwasher on a site unsuitable for any type of construction and under the direction of a family that had to invent a new type of concrete to make it happen.

*The artist had to develop a slow-setting concrete to create
the figures at the Shrine of St. Joseph in Yarnell.*

Back in the 1940s the Wasson family decided to build a
statue of St. Joseph on the rock-strewn hills half a mile from
downtown Yarnell. So they set out to find Felix Lucero, a sculptor, because they had read about his work. They found him
washing dishes in a Tucson restaurant and asked him to come
work on their project. First, however, they had to tinker with
the formula for concrete, the only material they could afford. It
had to be particularly slow setting, because the statue was to be
placed in a hard-to-get-at location.

Once the statue was finished, the Wassons kept the sculptor
on, and the shrine was expanded to include five other works
depicting the life of Jesus Christ. The sculptures were placed

among huge granite boulders, and irregular stairways were anchored to the slope. It's an easy hike but a little bit difficult for the short of breath, the out of shape, and the pot of bellied.

The shrine, located about half a mile west of Highway 89 as it passes through Yarnell, is open daily during daylight hours. There's no charge and there's no address. For more information, log on to www.stjoseph-shrine.com.

THE ELEPHANT'S SECRET
Yarnell

Everyone here knows about the Yarnell Hill Elephant and where to find it, but nobody knows how it got there. A lot of people think they know, but they all have a different story or theory.

This much is fact: The elephant is white. It was painted onto a rock at a hairpin bend on Highway 89 3 miles south of Yarnell. Because the road is divided as it passes through that stretch, only southbound travelers can see the pachyderm. It's not a complete elephant; the original artist apparently ran out of paint or rock surface, so only the front half is finished.

Things get a little hazy after that. One of the more popular stories is that a circus wagon carrying an elephant tipped over near the spot. Some say the elephant died, so the painting is a memorial. Others say it lived, so the silhouette is a tribute.

There's also a version that says the painting is the work of a highway-department employee who put it there to warn motorists about the treacherous curve. But others claim the highway department doesn't like the painting and has even painted over it because it's considered a distraction for motorists trying to maneuver the curve. And some say three high-school students rendered the artwork as a token of appreciation after safely traversing the road.

Despite such lack of clarity, the elephant has become a symbol of the community, and the residents have become its caretakers. Whenever the creature needs a new coat of paint, persons unknown apply it. If vandals deface it, somebody mysteriously removes the graffiti. The elephant carries a red heart on its trunk every February 14, and it's always gone the next day. And small Christmas decorations show up on its back every December.

The people of Yarnell don't consider it a mystery at all, however. It's just the way things happen.

Life on the Tee
Yucca

Hank and Ardell Schimmel live in a golf ball.

Their home is round and it's perched atop an iron standpipe, so it looks like a giant golf ball sitting on a tee waiting to get smacked by a driver.

A really, really, really big driver.

The structure is a 40-foot geodesic sphere, originally built as a nightclub and restaurant for a land-development project. The Schimmels bought it in 1981, after the development went bankrupt. They took up residency in 1991 and went to work converting it from an empty shell into their home by dividing it into three floors. The kitchen and den are on the first level, dining and living rooms on the second, and bedrooms on the third. There's a full bath on each floor, and the total living area is 3,400 square feet.

Hank and Ardell Schimmel live in constant fear that a giant golfer armed with an oversized driver may someday spot their home.

To give the place a little more offbeat character, they also added flying saucers, including one that measured 30 feet across. That one had to go, they said, because it was causing traffic problems on Interstate 40, which passes just a few hundred feet from their front yard.

The Schimmels have to be in good shape. There are forty-two steps leading from the ground to the first level, another twenty up to the second story, and eighteen more to reach their bedrooms. A huge circular enclosure surrounds the standpipe. It was designed to be a swimming pool, but nobody ever filled it. "It'd take an awful lot of water," Hank Schimmel observed.

The couple moved here from Wyoming, where they owned RV parks, hotels, and restaurants. They found the sphere during a winter visit, and Hank presented it to his wife as a birthday present. "He's always buying something goofy," she said.

The golf ball home is on Alamo Road just south of Yucca.

SOUTHEAST

SOUTHEAST

TOME ON THE RANGE
Benson

Winn Bundy doesn't care much for convention. This may explain why her Singing Winds Bookshop is located on a cattle ranch out in the flatlands and far from the nearest town, in direct violation of the prime business directive, "Location, Location, Location."

Although visitors have to travel a dirt road to get there, the place is a major draw. An average of fifty people per day take exit 304 off Interstate 10 at Benson, go north on Singing Wind Road, turn right at the shot-up old mailbox, open the gate, go through the gate, close the gate so the cattle don't wander off the property, and head on up to the ranch house.

Bundy and her late husband ignored common sense and advice from business consultants when they opened the shop in 1974 with about $600 worth of books. "It was awful nervy of us," Bundy admits. "We had two shelves of books and were calling ourselves a bookstore."

But the little shop prospered and grew. The living room was converted into book display space. So was her husband's workshop. When the children left home, their bedrooms were put to this new use. Now there are books everywhere—on shelves and racks, in nooks and crannies, over the doors and on the floors.

The store has been the subject of articles in such prestigious publications as the *Wall Street Journal, Time, National Geographic Traveler* and *Arizona Highways,* and many of its visitors are from foreign countries.

Bundy also raises cattle and supervises the ongoing additions to the bookshop, which is also still her home. And when she needs a break, she goes outside and plays basketball. She doesn't volunteer her age, but a newspaper clipping displayed on a wall refers to her as "a 59-year-old grandmother." The clipping is dated 1989.

For more information and directions, call (520) 586–2425. And don't forget to shut the gate.

IN-HOUSE STARGAZING
Benson

The Skywatcher's Inn is a bed-and-breakfast that promises the sun, the moon, and the stars and can actually deliver.

Pat and Eduardo Vega own and operate the combination guest house, observatory, and nature retreat east of Benson. Anyone with a reservation is welcome but most guests have one thing in common—astronomy.

So the facility is equipped with some of the finest sky-watching equipment in the world, including a 12-inch Schmidt-Cassegrain telescope, a 20-inch Maksutov telescope, a dome that opens, a change-coupling device, imaging capabilities, and a 14.5-inch Newtonian telescope.

It didn't start out that way. It was supposed to be a farm. Pat Vega is a country girl from Ohio; her husband is an amateur astronomer from the Dominican Republic. She wanted to go back to the farm; he wanted to devote more time to astronomy.

So they purchased 65 acres, bought some animals and telescopes and pretty soon, folks began dropping by.

Interest reached such an intensity that the couple decided to open a bed-and-breakfast. They expanded the farmhouse, which now features three bedrooms, a small studio, two kitchens, a science classroom, media room, library, and elegant living and dining rooms. Astronomers and others who visit can listen to lectures by Pat Vega or hire a staff astronomer for private sessions.

The farm is still operational, but twenty acres of the original spread has been converted into a riparian area complete with hiking paths and bird-watching stations.

Interested stargazers can visit www.communiverse.com/sky watcher or call (520) 586–7906.

A CAVERNOUS SECRET
Benson

The Kartchner Caverns are, in a word, spectacular. A 2.5-mile passageway connects two large rooms more than 100 feet high and 300 feet long. Over the eons, chemical reactions created an underground landscape that rivals computerized depictions of distant planets.

Dripping water and the other chemicals carved the rooms out of the limestone base and then filled them with such wondrous formations as stalactites and helictites and covered the walls with colors so brilliant they are often compared to tapestry.

The caverns are now an Arizona state park that draws more than 180,000 visitors a year and has created a mini-economy of hotels and restaurants in the surrounding area. But even more amazing is the story of two young men who kept their mouths shut to protect it.

Randy Tufts was eighteen when he stumbled across a sink-hole in the Whetstone Mountains in 1967. He briefly explored it but never returned to the site until 1974, when he brought his friend Gary Tenen along. They got into the caverns by squirming through several cracks that led to the splendor below. But fearful that vandals and curious cavers would over-run the treasure, they told no one about their discovery.

The pair kept their secret for almost four years before revealing it to the Kartchner family, owners of the property. They worked together to preserve the caverns by maintaining their silence; they finally went public in 1988 after the state bought the land and made plans to protect it.

Randy Tufts died in 2002 at the age of fifty-three.

The caverns, located on State Route 90 9 miles south of Benson, are open daily except Christmas. There is an admission fee and reservations are mandatory. For more information, call (520) 586–2283 or (520) 586–4100.

HOME IS WHERE THE AIRSTREAM IS
Bisbee

The Shady Dell Trailer Court is neither shady nor delled. It is, instead, a museum that exists primarily to prove the theorem that if somebody collects something, somebody else will come to look at it. Or, in this case, to stay in it.

The collection is old travel trailers, aluminum-bodied taga-longs from as far ago as the 1930s. Ed Smith and Rita Person-ett, the owners, started it in 1995 when they bought a homemade unit and hauled it back from California. They then acquired two more and bought a trailer park, which they renamed the Shady Dell.

Need a good night's sleep in a tin trailer? The Shady Dell Trailer
Court in Bisbee offers accommodations in restored travel trailers,
plus meals at Dot's Diner.

At first Smith didn't look at the acquisitions as a financial
venture. He planned to restore the trailers and put them on display as an art project. But Personett saw it as a business
endeavor, so they cleaned up the trailers they had, bought
more, and opened them as mini–guest houses. They also purchased an old diner that now serves their clientele.

Their guests stay in such old-timers as a 1949 Airstream, a
'57 El Rey, or a '51 Spartan Mansion. Or in a cabin cruiser sitting on blocks, or an old bus. Each unit has been painstakingly
restored, from the Melmac dishes in plywood cupboards to the
dial radios sitting on Formica countertops to the knickknacks

on the walls. Aluminum lawn chairs sit on small patios, and a couple of the units even feature the obligatory plastic flamingo.

If sleeping in cramped quarters is your kind of fun, call Ed or Rita at (520) 432-3567. Reservations are required.

FOCUS ON THE PIT
Bisbee

If you've ever used a kitchen spoon to dig for gold in the backyard or wondered how long it'd take to shovel your way to China, the Lavender Pit may be your personal mecca. It's a big hole in the ground, dug over a twenty-three-year span as part of a copper mining operation. It's wider than anything you ever scooped out with Mom's best soup ladle, deeper than anything you ever imagined while burying your mad money behind the garage.

Many retired backyard diggers make pilgrimages here to stare and make profound statements like, "Boy, that thing sure would hold a lot of beer." Then they whip out their cameras or video recorders, intent on capturing the magnitude of this inverse mountain so they can show it to the folks back home. But in the end, most are defeated by the very enormity they so admire. It's so big you can't take a picture of it.

Too bad. It would make a good picture, because the pit is humongous—1,000 feet deep, .75 mile wide, 1.5 miles long, and covering 600 acres. From 1951, when it opened, until 1974, when it was shut down, men and machines dug 375 million tons of material out of it. That figure included 94 million tons of ore, 108 million tons of leach material, and 173 million tons of waste rock.

The pit, named after former Phelps-Dodge official Harrison Morton Lavender Sr., was also responsible for obliterating a town. Before mining operations began, the 191 homes and businesses that made up the community of Lowell had to be relocated.

The Lavender Pit is located on State Route 80 about a mile from downtown Bisbee. You can't miss it.

THE GREAT HUFFANDPUFF
Bisbee

There's nothing flat about Bisbee. Almost every structure in town was built into a hill, on top of a hill, or at the foot of a hill, so they cling precariously to slopes and downward turns. As a result the city has lots of outdoor staircases, and thousands of stairs lead to both homes and business places.

Because they were built about a hundred years ago, some of the staircases began deteriorating. Rather than let an important segment of their history crumble, the citizens of Bisbee organized the Great Stair Climb to raise money for stair preservation.

The event, which started in 1990, combines running, walking, and climbing 1,034 stairs, which means there's also probably a lot of huffing, staggering, puffing, reeling, and collapsing involved. According to the registration form, "it's a 5K that feels like a 10K (and) a wonderful way to tour Old Bisbee."

For those who want to elevate their masochism to a higher level, there's the Barco IceMan competition. Contestants are timed as they run up 153 stairs. Carrying an eight-pound block of ice. Held in ice tongs and slung across their backs.

The stair climb is held in mid-October. For more information on how to get rid of that beer belly in one afternoon, check the Web site at www.bisbeestairclimb.org, or write to Save Our Stairs, P.O. Box 1099, Bisbee, AZ 85603.

WHERE LEGENDS ARE BORN
Bonita

After operating for more than one hundred years, the Bonita Store has closed its doors. Chain-link fencing surrounds the old building, and its windows now stare vacantly at the past. There are many tales about the store and the wide-open spaces that encompass it. One is particularly interesting because it involves Billy the Kid and his first victim.

The locals don't claim the incident actually occurred in the store itself, but they say it was definitely somewhere in the vicinity. According to legend and a smattering of fact, it happened this way.

He was known as Henry McCarty at the time and worked as a cook, wrangler, and horse thief at Camp Grant, a couple of miles away from Bonita. On the night of August 17, 1877, McCarty got into a bar fight with F. P. "Windy" Cahill, the local blacksmith. One witness said Cahill was getting the best of the fight when "the Kid" pulled out a pistol and shot his antagonist, who died the next day.

McCarty fled Arizona and never returned. He moved to New Mexico, changed his name to William Bonney, and eventually was gunned down by Sheriff Pat Garrett on July 14, 1881. Although many historians have branded him as a cold-blooded killer, others say he was responsible for only five or six deaths, including Cahill's.

There's not much left in Bonita, just the old store and some ranch houses. The store served as a saloon, gathering place, and mercantile for a century. Its demise signals the end to another chapter of the Old West.

Folklorists and those who don't believe that Billy the Kid was accurately portrayed by Chuck Courtenay in the unforgettable movie *Billy the Kid vs. Dracula* can still visit the site, however. Bonita is on State Route 266 off Highway 191 southwest of Safford.

INCARCERATION FOR THE INCARCERATOR
Clifton

It's not much to look at, just a hole in the wall, but Clifton's first jail has a couple of notable facets. One deals with its construction. The other deals with its first occupant.

The jail was built in 1881. Actually, "built" is not a good description. It was hacked, hammered, and drilled into a hillside. When completed, it was nothing more than a hole surrounded by solid rock and iron bars. This made escape relatively difficult.

Local legend says the first prisoner was Margarito Verala, the man who built the jail. When the job was finished, he converted his paycheck into large amounts of distilled spirits, shot up the town, was arrested, and was thrown into the rock prison he had created. Local legend doesn't go into any detail about how long he was incarcerated.

The jail is across the street from the old railroad depot on State Route 75 as it passes through the downtown area. It's easy to spot because there's a non-functioning railroad locomotive sitting next to it.

THE ART OF FLOOD PREVENTION
Clifton

The southern portions of Clifton suffered major flood damage when the San Francisco River overran its banks twice in the 1970s and again in 1983. To remedy that, the Army Corps of Engineers and the State of Arizona developed a levee system to serve as a flood-control project. But the levee had to cross State Route 75, which also serves as Clifton's main street. For obvious reasons, that created a problem.

So the government agencies authorized construction of a huge gate that would be open most of the time but that would automatically close whenever the river ran wild. The levee walls are thick concrete, so they're not much to look at. But the gate itself is a work of art.

It stands about 12 feet tall, measures 25 feet across, and weighs an estimated 5 tons. The panels of rusted iron and corrugated steel are designed to resemble the mountainous landscape that surrounds the community.

The locals have dubbed it "the Jurassic Park Gate," and some aren't impressed. Others, however, defend it. "Those people who don't care for it now will sure like it the next time the river floods," said local newspaperman Walter Mares.

So, does it work?

It has functioned properly during trial runs, but Arizona has been in the throes of a severe drought since the mid-1990s. The San Francisco River has been reduced to a trickle, so the gate has never been tested under real-life conditions.

ROLLING WITH THE THUMPS
Coolidge

Cotton-bale rolling is one of those sports that may never produce multimillion dollar superstars. There are a couple of good reasons. One is that the contestants don't get to knock anybody down. Another is that cotton bales are very hard to roll; they're rectangular, so they have corners.

Nonetheless, teams of cotton-bale rollers suit up every year to participate during Coolidge Cotton Days, an annual event held to observe the area's cotton industry. Competitors are divided into age brackets, from three years old to adult. The bales range from 11.5 pounds for the kiddies to 550 pounds for the grown-ups.

And remember, all the bales are rectangular. "Once you start rolling, they sort of hop," said Candy Hastings, director of the Coolidge Chamber of Commerce, which sponsors the event. "You have to catch them just right or they hop back at you."

The bale rollers are timed as they roll their bales over a 50-yard course. Adult winners get cash prizes; youngsters receive merchandise.

If bowling or pushing rhinos over is getting a little too tame for you, call the Coolidge chamber at (520) 723–3009 for details on bale rolling, and start a new career.

THE PROTECTED PROTECTOR
Coolidge

The center of attraction at the Casa Grande Ruins National Monument is a 4-story caliche structure that was built around A.D. 1300. The building has held up fairly well, considering it sat outdoors in the blistering sun and limited rainfall for more than seven centuries before anyone decided it was worth saving.

After declaring the ruins a national monument, the federal government erected a huge steel roof over the original building. That was in 1932, and the total cost was about $28,000. The roof protects the ruins from the elements but in so doing, it has also become a target of the sun, wind, and rain. So it needs repairs and repainting every now and then.

Somewhere along the line, the roof was placed on the National Register of Historic Places, which makes it subject to many of the same rules as the ruins when it comes to upgrades. So when the roof needed patching a few years ago, the procedure required special equipment and materials. For example, the solder used in the original construction is no longer manufactured, so the repair crews had to get special permission to use a substitute.

The huge parasol will have to be repainted in 2003, according to Don Spencer, the superintendent at the monument. "The bill was $29,000 the last time we painted it," he said. "That's more than it cost to build it. I don't even want to think of how much it'll be this time."

For a fee, steel-umbrella fans can view the roof and the monument it protects daily from 8:00 A.M. to 5:00 P.M. It's just north of Coolidge on State Route 287.

MOW, MOW, MOW YOUR BOAT

In the 1920s the federal government decided Arizona needed another dam. Surveyors picked a site on the San Carlos Apache Reservation and when the barrier was completed, they named it Coolidge Dam after the incumbent president.

Calvin Coolidge himself showed up for the dedication, along with several other dignitaries and humorist Will Rogers. Unfortunately for the celebrants, there was very little water in the impound behind the dam. The main water source, the Gila River, had all but dried up due to an extended drought.

But the ceremony went ahead anyway. President Coolidge was his usual taciturn self during his presentation and didn't say anything all that memorable. And when it was Rogers' turn to speak, he looked out over the field of weeds and observed, "If that was my lake, I'd mow it."

A COLLECTOR'S MUSEUM
Dos Cabezas

Orville Mickens said right off that he's a collector. "I've been picking up stuff around here for more than sixty years," he said while unlocking the door to his Frontier Relics Museum. "Most of this is from forts, ghost towns, and old mines."

Despite its remote location, Orville Mickens' museum at Dos Cabezas attracts tourists, sometimes even by the busload.

Once inside, Mickens pointed with pride to his assortment of calf blabbers, once used to wean calves, and frozen Charlottes, small porcelain statuettes that replaced candles on birthday cakes. He has opium bottles used by Chinese laborers, Civil War attire, arrowheads, old rifles and pistols, newspaper clippings, and books he uses to research his finds.

His prize possession is a brass conquistador's stirrup that he says dates from about 1540. It is in near-perfect condition because it was found in a cave. Nearby hangs a sword from the same era but not in very good shape because it has been exposed to the elements.

Mickens said his days as a collector may be past because many of the places he used to probe are now regulated and off-limits. So now he's a curator, giving personal tours to anyone who stops and honks like it says on the sign in the parking lot. There's no fee, and if you pay attention and remain interested, he'll open the other half of the museum and show you the 1950 Cadillac he restored.

The Frontier Relics Museum is on State Route 186 about 14 miles south of Willcox. Call (520) 384-3481 to make sure Orville will be there to show you around.

A PLACE TO GET MARILYNED
Douglas

When Vanessa Quintana hung a couple of photographs of Marilyn Monroe on the walls of her Mexican and American restaurant, she had no idea it would turn into a shrine for the blond sex symbol. But customers began contributing other pictures and, little by little, the number of photos, posters, and other Marilyn-related representations reached near-monumental proportions.

Now one entire wall and a stairwell in the Grand Café are covered with Marilyn art. Since they're not lined up in orderly fashion, it's difficult to count them over a chicken enchilada, but it looks like there are more than 200 items. They range from a life-size cutout of the star at the head of the stairs to movie lobby cards written in French, German, and Spanish. About the only thing missing is the famous calendar photo that shows Marilyn wearing only a come-hither look.

Vanessa Quintana no longer resides in Douglas, but she returns for big functions such as Halloween, to dress up like Marilyn and make guest appearances in parades and at her restaurant.

The Grand Café is at 1119 G Avenue in downtown Douglas. The phone number is (520) 364-2344, but don't expect Marilyn to sing "Happy Birthday" if you call.

WHERE PANCHO VILLA RODE

*T*he lobby of the 140-room Gadsen Hotel looks like it was transplanted from somewhere in Europe. It features an elegant white Italian marble staircase, four soaring marble columns topped by capitals decorated in 14-carat gold leaf, and a balcony that surrounds the entire second story.

But a lot of people visit the hotel to look at a flaw. One of the steps is chipped.

According to local folklore, the infamous Mexican bandit Pancho Villa found the staircase so appealing that he rode his horse to the top. "It's a legend that's been around forever," said Robin Brekhus, one of the owners. "There's nobody alive anymore who can officially back it up, but people have been telling the story for almost a hundred years. And there is that chip on the seventh step. The old-timers claim it was knocked out by the horse."

Villa had been fighting in the Agua Prieta area just across the Arizona border in Mexico when the hotel was built in 1907, and many residents of Douglas claim they're descendants of people who actually witnessed the equestrian stair climb. The staircase and columns survived a fire that destroyed most of the hotel in 1927. It was rebuilt of structural steel and reinforced concrete and reopened in 1929.

S I T E   F O R   S A N C T I T Y
Douglas

T he most interdenominational block in the world may be
Church Square, located a short distance from downtown
Douglas. There's a church on every corner. It's been that way
for almost a century, and there's no indication it'll ever change.

The Grace United Methodist Church was built on the northwest corner in 1902. The next year local Episcopalians erected
St. Stephen's Episcopal Church on the northeast corner, and
that was followed by completion of the First Baptist Church on
the southwest corner in 1904. The quartet was completed when
the First Presbyterian Church was finished in 1907.

The square takes up the block bounded by Tenth and
Eleventh Streets and D and E Avenues. The four churches still
hold regular services, and the people who attend claim the block
is the only one in the world with a church on every corner.

J U S T   H O R S I N '   A R O U N D
Dragoon

I f the name doesn't pique your interest, the function will. The
name is And the Horse You Rode In On; it's an equestrian
bed-and-breakfast located in the foothills of the Dragoon Mountains. The establishment is situated on six hundred acres of
high desert and has fourteen rental units.

The difference between this lodging place and most others is
that ten of the units are for horses. Guests can trailer their steeds

to the ranch, have them put up in one of the stalls, and not worry about feeding them or cleaning up behind them. That's all in the $6.00 per-night fee. So are two meals a day. Owners may bring their own horse food, but the cost is the same.

Humans don't get by so cheaply. Rates run from $70 to $85 per night, depending on occupancy, and they get only the wake-up meal. But having someone else clean the paddock has to be worth something.

Deborah and Will Scott, both attorneys in Tucson, are the founders and owners of the ranch, and they have named each of the four human guest suites after one of their own horses.

Guests and their horses can ride through the ranch's six hundred acres or the nearby Coronado National Forest. Those without horses can hike, bike, or rent a horse from an adjacent ranch.

And The Horse You Rode In On B&B is located about 65 miles east of Tucson off Interstate 10. For more information on where to get two meals a day and a clean paddock, log on to www.horseyourodeinon.com, or call (520) 826–5410.

NICE PLACES TO LIVE, BUT NOT TO DIE FOR
Eden and Paradise

The idea of going to a far, far better place after departing this world holds a certain appeal to many, but those planning to get a head start by being interred in Eden or Paradise may run into complications. Both are very small communities in southeastern Arizona, and both have cemeteries. But getting buried there is not simply a matter of showing up in a hearse.

The Eden cemetery is reserved for those who die while living in the community, those who once lived there, or those who have relatives already buried there. The cemetery board had to draw up the covenants because there were too many requests for plots. It was economics, not the lure of getting closer to Heaven, that caused the restriction. It costs less to get buried in Eden than any of the other cemeteries in the Gila River Valley.

Over in Paradise, similar laws govern who gets to molder in the graves of Paradise Cemetery. The cemetery association had to place limits on occupancy because there are too few spaces to fill all the requests of those who want to go to Paradise after death. So lots are allotted only to those who live there now or lived there once.

So the moral is: If you want to get to Paradise or Eden after death, you'd better stake your claim beforehand.

A S TOMPIN' G OOD T IME
E l g i n

Deep within the psyches of almost every human being, there lies a suppressed urge to jump into a vat of freshly picked grapes and stomp. Most never get to satisfy the urge but every now and then, a small window of opportunity opens.

One is at the Harvest of the Vine Festival staged on the last weekend of September by six wineries in southeastern Arizona. For the price of admission, guests can eat the food, taste the wine, hear the music, and stomp the grapes. But, alas, the nectar of their stompings will never see the inside of a wine cask. Only the juice of grapes stomped by a professional is used in the wine-making process.

That makes Gary Reeves, founder and owner of the Village of Elgin Winery, a rarity. He's the only wine maker in the state who stomps his own reds. During the annual harvest, Reeves said he stomps about one hundred tons of fruit. He admitted his feet get tired but added, "You gotta do what you gotta do."

For information on when and where to get your feet juiced, call (520) 455–9309.

LIONIZING MELVIN JONES
Fort Thomas

Distractions are few on this stretch of U.S. 70, where Mount Graham is a bluish gray mass on the horizon, and a few other peaks rise gently from the flatlands.

Otherwise, this two-lane stretch of asphalt zips through cotton fields and small villages without inspiration.

But suddenly there's a spire standing 50 feet above the semidesert all by itself with no church attached. Closer inspection reveals that it's a monument to Melvin Jones. Since a 50-foot obelisk doesn't just pop out of the ground all by itself, this poses a question: Who was Melvin Jones?

Melvin Jones isn't a household name unless you're a Lion. This obelisk near Fort Thomas honors the founder of the international service club.

The answer is obvious to the more than 1.6 million members of Lions International, a worldwide service organization with 45,000 clubs across the globe. Melvin Jones, the recognized founder of the Association of Lions Clubs, was born at Fort Thomas on January 13, 1879, the son of a U.S. Cavalry captain and his wife.

The Safford Lions Club financed the monument and dedicated it in 1965. There's also a small Melvin Jones Museum on the site, but it's open only once a year, on the Saturday closest to Jones' January 13 birth date. That's when Lions from all over the world gather to roar tribute to their founder.

The monument is on the north side of the highway. Those in need of a lion's share of information should call the Graham County Chamber of Commerce, (888) 837–1841.

MEMORIAL TO A FALLEN HERO
Along the Pinal Pioneer Parkway

Just north of Tom Mix Wash, at a rest stop between Mile Markers 15 and 16 on State Route 79 (also known as the Pinal Pioneer Parkway), there stands a rock monument topped by a steel silhouette of a riderless horse named Tony.

It is a memorial to Tom Mix, a movie cowboy whose career spanned both the silents and talkies. He died near the spot on October 12, 1940, in a one-car accident in the desert. He was sixty years old.

Mix made 370 movies and earned $20,000 a week at the peak of his career in the 1920s and 1930s. Before entering the movies, he served with the Texas Rangers, won a national rodeo championship, and worked as a hunting guide. After leaving the movies, he joined the circus and traveled across the country meeting his fans and performing tricks with Tony, his horse.

He was on an advance publicity campaign when he died. The bronze plaque on his memorial reads TOM MIX—JAN. 6, 1880— OCT. 12, 1940—WHOSE SPIRIT LEFT HIS BODY ON THIS SPOT AND WHOSE CHARACTERIZATIONS AND PORTRAYALS IN LIFE SERVED TO BETTER FIX MEMORIES OF THE OLD WEST IN THE MINDS OF LIVING MEN.

The monument is on the west side of the road about 15 miles south of Florence.

THE DESERT BLOOMS
In the Desert near Florence

St. Anthony's Greek Orthodox Monastery is an oasis in an otherwise flat piece of desert. In less than a decade, the monks who live there built two churches, four chapels, housing, maintenance facilities, rotundas, fountains, and sandstone walkways. They also planted thousands of trees, shrubs, and cactus, literally converting the once-barren desert into one of the most beautiful spots in Arizona.

Construction began in 1995; the first church was completed within a year. It is one of ten monasteries started in North America by Father Ephraim, a spiritual leader from the Greek Orthodox homeland at Mount Athos in Greece.

Surrounded by foliage and spires, visitors might easily envision themselves in a foreign country. The roofs and columns on the places of worship vary from copper domes to bell towers, and the architecture ranges from brick to stone to lumber.

Visitors are asked to check in at the bookstore directly inside the entryway, where they are welcomed with pitchers of ice water and sweet cakes. They may attend services, walk through the grounds, take photographs, and enter the churches.

The monks who built and reside at St. Anthony's Greek Orthodox Monastery
near Florence have turned a piece of desert into a bit of paradise.

But there are some restrictions. Men are asked to wear long pants and long-sleeved shirts. Women should wear skirts below the knees, long-sleeved shirts or blouses, and have their heads covered with a veil or scarf. No hats, caps, sheer scarves, shorts, pant-skirts, miniskirts, or sleeveless blouses. Everyone is asked to wear socks, especially when wearing sandals. A limited supply of proper attire is available in the bookstore for improperly clad guests. Smoking and conversation with the monks are not allowed.

To reach the monastery, take Paisano Road east off State Route 79 about 12 miles south of Florence. Stay on the paved road; it'll lead you directly to the entry.

PRISON PRODUCE
Florence

The Prison Arts Store and Trade Outlet is a one-of-a-kind boutique. Everything for sale in the store is made by inmates, either at the Arizona State Prison in Florence or similar lockups around the state.

Goods vary. There are wallets, crocheted hats, amateur oil paintings, wood carvings, horsehair hatbands, jewelry and jewelry boxes, scrimshaw, and, fittingly, novelty license plates.

Most of the revenue goes back to the inmates, but the Department of Corrections keeps a percentage for overhead. What's left is deposited into the inmates' personal bank accounts and can be used to purchase items within the prison, to support families, or to provide restitution to victims.

The store is housed in a small trailer at the intersection of State Route 79 and Butte Avenue, just west of the prison. It's open Friday through Monday. And forget all those commercials about bringing your credit card along. They only accept cash. For more information, call (520) 868–3014.

WHERE TIME STANDS STILL
Florence

All four faces of the clock on the old Pinal County Courthouse tower say 11:44 no matter what time of day it is. This is good because most people look at the clock during the daylight hours. So no matter what time it is, the clock says it's almost time for lunch.

The time has been stuck at 11:44 since the building opened in 1891, and it'll always be 11:44 because the hands never move. They're painted on. This was an economic move at first, but now it has become tradition.

There has never been a real clock in the courthouse. The architect built the tower because he wanted a clock on the building, but the board of supervisors at that time saw it as a frivolity and wouldn't approve money for the timepiece. So the hands were painted onto metal.

The courthouse is still in use as an adjunct to a newer facility, and it's undergone several remodeling and renovation procedures. Every time the place gets a face-lift, the fake clocks are repainted. This makes life a little easier for the people who work in the building. They don't have to wind the clock. And they don't have to wash the curtains on the third floor or clean the tower windows. They're painted on, too.

People who want to see what a permanent 11:44 looks like will find the courthouse at 135 North Pinal Street in Florence.

HAY! NICE PLACE YOU GOT THERE!
Florence

Bring on the wolf. He can huff and puff until his eye bones pop clear out of his head, but he's not going to blow this straw house down.

Actually, it's not a house. But then, the old story about the three piggy homebuilders probably has some misrepresentations in it, also.

The building is the Florence Senior Citizens Center, and a portion of it is built with straw. As part of a half-million-dollar remodeling project, three straw-bale walls were added to the old Town Library to create the center. The old section is adobe and was originally built in 1892 as a church. It then underwent several transitions before being converted into a partial house of straw.

The addition required 600 special bales that were cut late in the season to reduce moisture. The walls were sealed with stucco on the outside and plaster on the inside to give them an old adobe look. The procedure also makes them fireproof and, because the walls are 2 feet thick, there was no need to add insulation. Although straw-bale construction is not new, this was the first commercial building to use the technique in Arizona and New Mexico.

The center was named after longtime Florence resident Dorothy Nolan and is located at 330 North Pinal Street. You can go there and look but be careful how you say, "Hay you!"

JUST HANGIN' AROUND
Florence

The displays in the Pinal County Historical Museum range from furniture made of saguaro skeletons to books about Tom Mix to an old typewriter with two keyboards. One exhibit features a glass window with two bullet holes in it, the result of a shoot-out between a sheriff and his deputy. Another shows the many varieties of barbed wire used to tame the Old West.

But the exhibit that draws the most attention is located in the northwest corner of the museum and it's not for the squeamish. They call it the Arizona State Prison Collection, and what they have collected are nooses used to hang convicted murderers at the nearby state prison.

There are twenty-five nooses on display; they were used to hang twenty-seven men and one woman. The nooses are in cabinets, and each one encircles mug shots of its victims. The reason there are only twenty-five nooses for the twenty-eight hangings is that one noose was used four times because four convicts were executed on the same day.

The most infamous noose ended the life of Eva Dugan, who died on February 21, 1930. Due to a miscalculation on the weight of the condemned woman, she was decapitated. The gruesome spectacle caused the state legislature to rethink its execution policy, and lethal gas replaced hanging in 1933.

The museum, located at 715 South Main Street, is open from 11:00 A.M. to 4:00 P.M. Tuesday through Saturday, and from noon to 4:00 P.M. Sunday. But it closes from July 15 through August 31 and on major holidays.

A RATTLING SUCCESS
Gleeson

Finding Rattlesnake Crafts is somewhat akin to stumbling across a shrine dedicated to the discards of life. The business is located almost directly in the center of nowhere. But once you spot it, you'll know you've come to the right place. Your first remark will probably be something like, "Oh, for heaven's snakes!"

John and Sandy Weber own and operate the snake works, and they believe in using the whole snake. They hunt rattlesnakes with a 4-foot-long device they call "the snake stik" and then, when the critter has been disposed of, they use almost every part of it in their business. They make earrings and necklaces out of the vertebrae, rattles, and fangs; hatbands and ball-cap designs from the skin; paperweights and curios from the heads; and even a form of jerky from the meat.

They are required to obtain valid hunting licenses, they can't hunt some species, and they must limit their take of others. The Webers hunt only at night during the summer months and have never been bitten.

The couple quit their office jobs in Illinois and moved to the desert shortly after marrying in the early 1980s. Now their home is a modified travel trailer surrounded by a magnificent accumulation of used stuff, including cattle skulls, tin coffee pots, kitchen utensils, typewriters, machinery, tools, and gadgets. Many of the items hang from wires, so when the breezes pass by the entire area sounds like a giant wind chime. Quite a few of the relics came from area ranchers as barter. "It's a good deal," Weber said. "We give them snake crafts and they get rid of their junk."

Rattlesnake Crafts is located a mile and a half south of Glee-son Road, about 13 miles east of Tombstone. Look for the weathered old signs. Their e-mail address is misfitz@c212.com, and the phone number is (520) 642–9207.

DOUBLE-DUTY BILLBOARD
Globe

The way Rocky Miller sees it, there's no sense having a bill-board in your front yard if half of it is being wasted. To remedy that imbalance, he turned artist. Miller acquired the billboard several years ago as settlement of a lawsuit and rents out the front portion as signage to local merchants. But the backside wasn't very attractive; just bare panels and steel gray posts. Besides that, it blocked his view of downtown Globe.

So Miller took brush in hand. And now the reverse side is an oil-on-billboard creation, his interpretation of a log cabin sur-rounded by pine trees, animals, and a waterfall. It's not great art but it commands attention because of its size—42 feet by 12 feet, with four 12-inch steel poles embedded in concrete to hold it up.

"I painted it for my wife," Miller said. "We had a cabin on the Snake River and she's always been fond of it. Look at the way the animals' eyes follow you as you walk by. You don't see that in many paintings." Miller was age eighty-five when he com-pleted the work.

To view his panorama, take Haskins Terrace off Broad Street just east of the railroad underpass.

THE RUINS THAT AREN'T RUINED
Globe

Most ruins in Arizona are just that—ruins. Overseen by government agencies, they are stabilized but not rebuilt, because the philosophy is to preserve, not restore. That way of thinking sets the ancient Indian pueblo known as Besh-Ba-Gowah apart from the others. It has been partially rebuilt, and nobody's getting their nose all bent out of shape because of it.

Archaeologists trace its history from about A.D. 750 but say most of the construction went on between A.D. 1225 and 1400, when as many as 150 members of the Salado tribe may have lived there. The Apaches took control of the area after 1600 and kept it until the late 1800s. The name Besh-Ba-Gowah is a loose translation of "place of metal," the Apache term for the area.

After a couple of federal excavation projects in the early 1900s, the place went back to being a ruin until 1981, when the city took control and began a major restoration. Now it's an archaeological park, clean and neat and a testimonial to thousands of hours of volunteer labor. A couple of dwellings have been restored, using the same rocks as the original builders did.

The park is located at 150 North Pine. For details, call (520) 425-0320.

STAYING AFTER SCHOOL FOR FUN
Globe

L et's face it: We all want to go back to those glorious days of our youth when death and taxes weren't nearly as important as passing notes and chewing gum without getting caught. The Noftsger Hill Bed and Breakfast is one way to return, even though circumstances have changed.

The inn is an old schoolhouse, built in 1907. It served the community until 1981, then sat vacant for a decade before Pam and Frank Hulme bought it and started the lengthy restoration needed to convert it into a bed-and-breakfast. They got the job partially done, then sold the project to Dom and Rosalie Ayala, who have continued the reconstruction and now have six suites open. Five of them are former classrooms, so sleeping in school is, in this case, no longer a crime punishable by staying after school to clean blackboard erasers.

The classroom suites are large because they once held as many as forty-five children. The chalkboards are still on the walls and covered with comments from guests, many of them former students. The tiny rooms that served as coat closets are now bathrooms, and the janitor's closet is a smaller rental called the Cowboy Suite. Guests eat a home-cooked breakfast in one of the old administration offices.

And there's no extra homework if you accidentally sleep late and miss morning roll call. For details, call (877) 780–2479 or log on to www.noftsgerhillinn.com.

DOUBLE-CROSSED IN COCHISE COUNTY
Hereford

Seventy-five-foot Celtic crosses are rare in Arizona because they're hard to come by and hard to put up. It takes a crane and several skilled workers to install one properly so it doesn't fall and make a 75-foot dent in the ground. All that gives Cochise County double bragging rights, because there are two 75-footers within its boundaries.

One stands at the Holy Trinity Monastery, a Benedictine community at St. David. The other rises from a hillside near Hereford, about 40 miles away. Both are the result of a 1990 visit to a shrine in Medjugorje, Yugoslavia, by Gerry and Pat Chouinard. The couple owned property in Hereford and planned a retirement home there. After visiting Yugoslavia, they decided to include a shrine in their building plans.

Their original design had a huge cross and a 31-foot statue of the Virgin Mary rising side by side. But zoning officials wouldn't give their blessing because the cross and statue were ruled accessory structures that couldn't stand alone. The couple expanded their plans to include a chapel and acquired all the necessary permits. Then the neighbors complained, causing a series of lawsuits that took more than a year to settle.

But the cross was already done. Concerned about the delays, the Chouinards gave that work to the Benedictine monastery, where it was erected and dedicated in 1998. Meanwhile, back on the hillside, a Superior Court judge ruled that the original permits were legitimate and granted approval for the shrine.

So the Chouinards ordered another cross, plus the statue of Mary. Both crosses and the statue are made of structural steel covered with concrete and glass fiber. The small chapel, made

After surviving lengthy court battles, two 75-foot
crosses watch over both ends of Cochise County.

of river rock, features a large mural and huge wooden beams
that were originally part of a church in Michigan. The fourteen
Stations of the Cross are placed along the pathway that leads
from the parking lot to the building.

Our Lady of the Sierras Shrine is open to visitors of all
faiths. It's located in Ash Canyon, just beyond mile marker 333
on Arizona 92, about 8 miles south of Sierra Vista. Turn right
onto Ash Canyon Road and then left onto Twin Oaks Road, and
take Twin Oaks to the parking lot. For details, call (928)
378–2950.

SERVING THE LONELY
Klondyke

Bonnie Garwood and her daughter, Leslie, felt the need to be alone, so they bought the town of Klondyke. It wasn't like purchasing Manhattan for $24, of course, but they did acquire the general store, gift shop, video rental shop, restaurant, snack stop, real-estate office, gas station, off-sale liquor outlet, and what used to be the post office. That's not a really big deal, however, because they're all in the same building.

It's called the Klondyke Store, and it's perfectly positioned right in the middle of nowhere. The mother and daughter bought it in 1999 to get away from the hustle of the Phoenix area. Now they sell basic foodstuffs and cowboy hats to neighboring ranchers, hunters, bird-watchers, and folks who take the wrong turn.

They also own and operate the nearby Horsehead Lodge, which can accommodate thirteen guests, more if they're willing to sleep on the floor. Business is good. Besides being in the middle of a whole lot of peace and quiet, the lodge is near Aravaipa Canyon, a prime bird-watching spot; the Galiuro Wilderness Area; the Coronado National Forest; the Pinaleno Mountains; and the Santa Teresa Mountains.

Klondyke was founded in the early 1900s by a couple of spelling-challenged prospectors who had participated in the Klondike gold rush in the Yukon and wanted something to remind them of the experience, but in a warmer climate. The community grew to around 500 in the late 1920s; now the census is much easier to take—the permanent population is 4.

Get-away-from-it-allers, birders, and serenity seekers can reach Klondyke by turning off U.S. 70 onto the Aravaipa-Klondyke Road east of Fort Thomas. It's a gravel road but fairly well maintained. For more information, log on to www.klondykestore.com or call (877) 728-3335.

DUAL-CARBED TWIN-CAMMED DINOSAURS
Klondyke

To the untrained eye, John Franzone's art studio might look like a junkyard, due to the large number of old cars and a diverse assortment of old car parts that occupy his acreage. The cars are in various stages of disembowelment and the innards are sorted into large piles of transmissions, engines, oil pans, gears, and manifolds.

But there are works of art in every pile. Franzone is a sculptor and car parts are his medium. His works range in size from miniature World War I airplanes crafted from spark plugs to huge dinosaurs that require a flatbed truck to move them.

Franzone, who started this career in 1989 when he bought ten acres in the middle of this wilderness, had been an auto mechanic before. "Even back then," he said, "I'd look at a water pump and see beauty in it. The others looked at me like I was crazy."

His first effort was a plant stand composed of a brake drum, water pump, and transmission shaft. He sold it for $40 and became a full-time artist. Now he makes junkyard dogs from shock absorbers, mobiles from drive shafts, and dinosaurs from timing chains, fan blades, and oil pans. He acquires his materials by hauling in abandoned cars or buying junked parts from auto-repair shops.

Franzone's place is way out in the country so before heading there, be sure there's a full tank of gas in your car. Otherwise it might become part of the decor in somebody's home.

Take the Aravaipa-Klondyke Road off U.S. 70 east of Fort Thomas; follow that road south to the Klondyke Store, then go west for about 5 miles. Don't be afraid of the dinosaur guarding the front gate. It's only an old Ford pickup.

THE PRACTICE OF ECOWLOGY
Miami

If the tradition of erecting monuments to recognize great
deeds ever reaches this mining community, there might someday be a statue of a giant cow pie on the town's main street. It
was cow pies, after all, that brought life to the tailings.

Tailings are worthless soil, the result of earth that has been
pulverized to extract copper, the community's economic base for
more than a century. Mountains of tailings looked down on the
area, some rising 220 feet above the main street. They were an
ugly but necessary by-product of the mining process. Tailings
had become a part of Miami's landscape, contributing dust
when it was windy and milky ooze when it rained.

But then in the mid-1990s, along came the flosbies—four-
legged organic-soil-building industrial engineers—more commonly known as cows. A couple of agricultural engineers from
nearby Globe approached Cyprus Miami Mining with a pro-
posal that utilized cows, cow food, digestion, and natural
process (the politically correct wording for cow droppings) as a
method of restoring life to the sterile slopes.

The mining company terraced the tailings and added topsoil.
The cows were turned loose on the side hills, and they did what
cows normally do—eat, digest, and release fertilizer. Eventually
the bugs came. Birds followed, then small animals, and they all
contributed until the hills turned green.

The mining company took control of the project and
acquired a cattle ranch to provide its own livestock. Phelps
Dodge later bought Cyprus Miami Mining and has continued
the program. And, although the grass on the hills has turned
brown due to an extended drought, the vegetation has been

established, and it holds down the dust so local residents hail the experiment as an unqualified success.

The flosbied hills are visible from almost any vantage point in the twin cities of Miami and Globe. There are no plans to erect a monument to a cow plop, however.

NEITHER RAIN NOR ETC.

*E*arly land developers had to be ingenious when it came to selling lots. Consider this example from A History of the Miami Arizona Area, *compiled and adapted by W. A. Haak for the Gila County Historical Society:*

"No institution in Miami has had a more colorful career than the Miami Post office. . . . In December 1909, the post office was located in a little green frame building that could be hauled on a truck. The idea of putting the post office on wheels was originated by Mr. Van Dyke and Mr. Prochaska. They would station it at one corner and sell all the surrounding lots. When the cleanup was made, they would move the mobile post office to another corner and proceed to sell the lots in that section of town. It was a novel idea in peddling real estate, as all buyers wanted property close to the post office. . . . "

THE MINE THAT ATE A TOWN
Morenci

If you've ever dug up your mother's garden with a toy scoop shovel and hauled the dirt away in a toy dump truck, you should come here and get a taste of what the real world is like.

The Morenci Mine, owned and operated by Phelps Dodge, is one of the biggest man-made holes in the world. It's so big— 2,500 feet deep, 2 miles across, and a 9-mile perimeter—it once swallowed up an entire town. Like the one that replaced it, the town was called Morenci. When it got in the way of the mine, the company built a new community, razed the old buildings, and quarried the land underneath. This was possible because Phelps Dodge owned the town as well as the mine.

Eating a town requires a big appetite and enormous utensils, and the mining company has them. Their scoop shovels stand more than 50 feet high, so tall it takes an elevator to get from the ground to the control room. The buckets, which weigh 80 tons empty, take bites that weigh 80 tons and measure 54 cubic yards.

To handle loads like that, the company also owns huge trucks that can hold almost 170 cubic yards of ore-bearing rock. The trucks are more than 20 feet tall, have a wheelbase of nearly 20 feet, and can hold more than 1,000 gallons of fuel, a necessity because they slurp fuel at the rate of four to five gallons per mile. The tires are 40 inches wide and 12 feet in diameter, and they cost about $20,000 each. And when they wear out, they're hauled away to the dump ground because nobody wants to buy a used tire so big that it takes a flatbed truck to carry it.

The company uses the big equipment to extract more than 800,000 tons of ore from the pit every day. Due to cutbacks, the mine no longer offers guided tours, but visitors can still drive around the rim during daylight hours. You'll notice right away that those trucks are absolutely huge, even from half a mile away. For more information, call (520) 865–4521.

O *n l y* I *n* H *u m e r i c a*

N o g a l e s

When Jesse Hendrix puts on a brunch, it's a spread for up to 15,000 guests. Fortunately for Hendrix and his wallet, those who show up don't eat much because they're hummingbirds.

The Hendrix home a few miles northeast of Nogales is on the flight path the tiny birds use on their annual migrations. And on a good day during the migration peaks, an estimated 10,000 to 15,000 birds stop in for a snack.

Hendrix uses 150 feeders and goes through about 1,600 pounds of sugar and 3,500 gallons of water every year. He mixes the sweet water in plastic containers and pours it into the feeders. He varies the colors, using red, yellow, blue, green, and orange as a dating system to make sure the juice doesn't spoil. "You can't leave it in the feeder for more than three days during hot weather," he said.

The hummingbirds also attract bees and humans. Hendrix has developed special anti-bee devices but allows humans to visit most anytime, as long as they call ahead to make sure he'll be there. Bird-watchers, scientists, film crews, and school groups are regular visitors. He has been the subject of National Geographic and BBC television specials and a *People* magazine article.

It all started by accident. "A hummingbird came by one day about fifteen years ago," Hendrix said. "I liked him and wanted him to come back, so I put out some food. The next day there were two birds, then four showed up."

Now scientists believe thousands of the hummers deviate from their migratory patterns to stop off at Jesse's place. The birds fly from as far north as Alaska to their winter homes in Mexico every fall, then reverse the pattern in the spring. The best time to see them in big numbers is the last week in August and first week in September. Since their wings flap at tremendous speeds, making it difficult to count them, the best way to figure out how many hummers are at the ranch at one time is to count their beaks and legs, then divide by three.

For details and a map of how to get there, log on to www.azwildbirds.com. There's no admission fee. No bathrooms, either. So Hendrix cautions those who plan a visit "to take care of that before they leave home."

THE LEGACY OF MARTIN SALTER
Oracle

Oracle isn't very big, but the community takes its art very seriously. This is best illustrated at the Oracle Public Library and the Pedestrian Parkway, where the works of Martin Salter are on display. Both are within a hundred yards of each other on the town's main thoroughfare.

The library grabs the attention of both casual passerby and local resident because of the mural that surrounds the parking lot. It uses a series of panels to trace Oracle's history, emphasizing such factors as the arts, mining, ranching, Hispanic, and Native American influences. Salter drew the original design and then recruited local artists and high-school students to do the painting.

Just up the road a giant lizard perches on a rock to welcome visitors to the Pedestrian Parkway. The lizard is also Salter's

Since it's more whimsical than frightening, the concrete-and-ceramic-tile lizard in Oracle produces only smiles.

work. It's made of concrete and ceramic tiles and is much more whimsical than frightening. The tiny park also contains two huge tile arrowheads also designed by Salter and created by eighty volunteers. Salter died in 1999; a small bench in the park is dedicated to him and his work.

And now, here's the interesting part: Salter was not an artist. He was a mining engineer who loved art and wanted his community to be a place of culture.

Oracle is on State Route 77 about 30 miles north of Tucson.

A GLASS-ENCASED FUTURE
Oracle

Biosphere 2 was constructed as one whopping big experiment. The huge glass structure covers 3.5 acres, stands 91 feet high at its tallest point, and contains a 25-foot-deep million-gallon ocean, a rain forest, a desert, a marsh, and a savanna.

The original intent was to determine how well humans could survive under artificial conditions. In the late 1980s, eight biosphereans were sealed inside with orders not to come out for two years. But there were problems with the mechanical functions and accusations that some of the inhabitants sneaked out occasionally. In the end, some deemed the project a success; others said it was a farce.

Biosphere 2 was opened to the public as a research and learning center in 1990. Columbia University became a partner in 1996 and has spearheaded a multitude of changes. New educational and research programs have been developed, and educators at the center relay information about discoveries all over the world through campus courses and the Internet.

The complex now offers sleepovers in a new hotel, conference facilities, and a restaurant. Biosphere 2 (called that because Earth is considered Biosphere 1) is no longer available for overnight stays, however.

Fans of living under glass will find Biosphere 2 just off State Route 77 about 30 miles north of Tucson at mile marker 96.5. There are guided tours and admission fees that vary with the seasons. For more information, call (800) 828–2462 or log on to www.bio2.columbia.edu.

ETERNAL FLICKERS
Patagonia

A small jog in the pavement south of Patagonia allows cars to pull off the main road. A large rock faces the turnout and a bullet-riddled metal plaque glued to the rock tells about Johnny Wade and the ranch he operated in the area a century ago.

Right behind the rock, a set of cement stairs leads to a small shrine built into a rock grotto. Several candles surround religious statues, flickering day and night, illuminating the grotto while their smoke turns the ceilings black.

The shrine has been there since the early 1940s. Juanita and Juan Telles, a local couple, built it and vowed to keep candles burning inside in exchange for the safe return of their son who was fighting in World War II. The son returned safely. Members of the family since moved and passed away, but the candles still burn in the shrine. The townspeople of Patagonia have taken it upon themselves to preserve the past and continue the devotion, so they tend to the candle lighting every day, making sure the flames never flicker away.

The shrine is just south of mile marker 16, about 2.5 miles south of Patagonia on State Route 82.

FOR THE WINGED WONDERS
Patagonia

Patagonia isn't very big, so it's not surprising that the Patagonia Butterfly Park isn't very big either. The park is about the size of a small backyard, a tiny bit of Shangri-la where some of nature's showiest creatures find comfort and safety.

It's near the old railroad depot that now serves as the community's city hall and was constructed in 1996 after the city council approved the formation of volunteer groups to raise money, seek gifts, and donate their time to the project. Don Wenig, a retired teacher and artist, led the effort, and the result is an appealing combination of purple and red flowers, pathways, and rock gardens.

Ceramic tiles mounted on old railroad ties describe some of the winged visitors. There are more than 700 species of butterflies in North America; about 200 species spend part of their summer vacations here. The colorful creatures usually show up around mid-June and hang out until mid-October. Not all at the same time, of course. It's a small park.

For best viewing times and other information, call the Patagonia Visitors Information Center at (520) 394–0060.

M i n i n g   a s   S i m p l e   a s
B l a s t ,   W h a c k ,   P i c k
P e r i d o t

Several roads lead to the world's largest deposit of peridot, and each is an adventure unto itself. They're all dirt and they all snake their way through the hills and gullies with no apparent purpose other than to rip the bottom off a low-slung vehicle. More than half of them don't actually lead to the mine; they simply lead to a road that will eventually wind up at the mine.

And once there the uninitiated probably won't recognize it as a mine, anyway. This is not a high-tech extraction process. It's just a gorge in the flatlands of the San Carlos Apache Reservation, mined by Apaches equipped with hammers, crowbars, and coffee cans.

Peridot is a green, transparent, semiprecious stone that was once popular among Egyptian royalty. It still commands a degree of respect in the gem world as one of two August birthstones. The only other places it's found are Egypt, New Mexico, and Hawaii. The claim that this is the largest deposit in the world has never been officially substantiated, but the Apaches haven't been challenged because nobody knows just how many stones are still buried under the reservation.

The mining is basic hardscrabble—a bulldozer pushes big rocks aside, and the miners dig around by hand to find the green stones, which are used primarily in jewelry making. On a good day they may fill their coffee cans to the halfway mark and make $50 to $100 per pound.

But tenderfoots and claim jumpers beware: There are no directions and even if you stumble across it, the mine is off-limits to nonresidents. The town of Peridot is easy to find, however. It's 17 miles east of Globe on U.S. 70.

DO-IT-YOURSELF GHOSTING
Pomerene

Jay Gammons lives out his dream on a flat spot in the desert foothills west of Pomerene Road. At first glance there's nothing dreamlike about the place. It's old and dilapidated. There's a single street, and it sure ain't paved with gold. Only the wind stumbles through the dirt and wanders between the ramshackle buildings, then drifts off and vanishes into the surrounding isolation.

And that's exactly the way Jay Gammons wants it.

He calls the place Gammons Gulch. It's a combination tourist attraction, museum, and movie set where old buildings go to be resurrected. In his younger days Gammons dreamed of owning a ghost town, but there were never any "Ghost Towns For Sale" listings in the classified ads. He found some in California and Arizona, but his bids for ownership were rejected; so, he decided to build his own. He's been working at it since 1970, and he still isn't done.

Gammons' dad was a movie-location expert who worked in both movies and television, so young Jay watched countless western movies. Eventually he grew up, plunked down $5,000 for a ten-acre chunk of desert, and went to work. During the next two decades, he acquired old buildings from surrounding communities, dismantled them, hauled the pieces back to his ghost town, and reconstructed them.

So while none of the nineteen buildings are technically authentic, most of the material in them is. So are the 7,500 relics he uses for decor, everything from a 1912 light bulb to a genuine honky-tonk-saloon piano.

Gammons and his wife, Joanne, moved into the reconstructed hotel in 1990. Their living quarters are part of the display area, however, so it's not uncommon to have tourists tromping through the kitchen while they're eating.

The Gulch is open from 9:00 A.M. to 5:00 P.M. Wednesday through Sunday. For more information, call (520) 212–2831 or check www.gammonsgulch.com on the Web.

THE BALLADEER'S BALLAD
Ramsey Canyon

If Arizona is going to have an official state balladeer, it's only logical that there should also be a place where he can hang out and sing his ballads. At least, Dolan Ellis figured it that way.

Ellis, one of the nine original members of the New Christy Minstrels, was appointed state balladeer in 1967 by then-Gov. Sam Goddard and has been re-appointed by every governor since. The official duties of the post are a bit vague, but Ellis performs regularly at state functions and has written more than 200 songs about the state.

"But one day, I went to the library to look for material on Arizona folklore, the collection of folk songs about Arizona," Ellis said. "There wasn't any. Where were all the songs? Where was my stuff?" Being the official state balladeer, he decided there should be a special place for works like that. And so the Arizona Folklore Preserve came into being.

A fifty-seat theater is the core of the complex. It opened in 2001 and is situated on a brook that runs through Ramsey Canyon and actually babbles. Ellis and other musicians and songwriters display their wares and talents in the facility, and they also make use of its audio-and-video recording studio. The project was a joint venture between Ellis and the University of Arizona South.

For information about spending time with an official state balladeer and listening to his brook babble, call (520) 378–6165.

IS THAT A CROCOGATOR OR AN ALLICROC?

On Old State Route 88

The creature in question is probably life-size but not scary enough to keep even the meekest of hoodlums off the property, if that was the intention. Folks around here simply call it the crocogator because its origins are lost in the passage of time.

The crocogator is a stone-and-mortar replication of something that looks like it belongs in a swamp in Florida or Africa. Obviously the work of an amateur, it has been snarling and grimacing at travelers and passersby for an estimated seventy years.

Its markings resemble neither crocodile nor alligator. The real ones are sort of greenish; this one's black with white polka dots. Old-timers say it was built for the owner of a service station that operated on the site in the 1930s. The station's been closed for years, but the crocogator maintains its vigil.

Rare reptile fans can find the creature by taking State Route 188 between Globe and Miami north for 4 miles, turning onto Old State Route 88, and going another mile. It's on the right, and it needs a new paint job.

THE BIG BLUE THING
Safford

The creature's name is really Zubaz, but nobody calls it that. Mostly it's known as "Old Blue" or "Blue Thing." This is probably because it's blue. It also has three legs and a crystal growing out of its head.

Zubaz stands in the observatory at Discovery Park, an ambitious multimillion-dollar science and nature project that opened in 1996 on the city's southwestern edge. The explanation for the alien presence reads: "Our first contact with an extraterrestrial at Discovery Park was made recently with Zubaz. He is believed to come from a dwarf brown star orbiting in Pegus 51."

But in reality, Zubaz is the product of a child's imagination. Before

Zubaz, also known as "the Blue Thing," is either a genuine no-doubt-about-it space alien or the product of a child's imagination. It has taken up residency in the observatory at Discovery Park in Safford.

the observatory opened, the center sponsored a contest in which area children were asked for their ideas of what space creatures look like. It was a logical endeavor, considering that Discovery Park sits at the foot of Mt. Graham, where massive telescopes will someday explore the outer regions of the universe.

Desiree Mattice of Pima submitted the winning design, which was then converted into a sculpture by Pima artist Shirley Hall. Despite the fact that only a selected few have ever seen actual space creatures, this one looks pretty real.

For the nonbelievers the observatory also contains a variety of items pertaining to the cosmos. They include scientific and theological explanations of how the universe was formed, a large telescope, a space shuttle, and listening posts where people can hear pulsars.

Discovery Park, located out where Twentieth Avenue comes to a dead end, also has a miniature train that hauls visitors around the 200-acre site. Hours are from 9:00 A.M. to 6:00 P.M. Friday and Saturday. For information, call (928) 428–6260.

A TRUNKATED ICON
Safford

Moffitt's New-To-U on the south side of Safford is a place where they sell stuff. Old stuff and used stuff. And stuff that people have absolutely no use for but they buy it anyway, because one never knows when there'll be an urgent need for plastic tortillas.

The establishment is well-known in the city, and it's easy to find because of the elephant sculpture that guards the front door. Quite a bit less than life-size, the work consists of a 275-gallon oil drum for the body, mud flaps for the ears, bull horns for the tusks, pieces of 6-inch-long steel pipe for the legs, dryer

*Shirley Moffitt stands next to an elephant of dubious
ancestry as it gives new meaning to "mastodontics" at her
New-To-U shop in Safford.*

hose for the trunk, and flexible tubing for the tail.

Its creator was Carl Hurleyman, who lived next door to the
Moffitts' place of business before his death in 1985. "He wanted
us to have something to remember him by," co-owner Shirley
Moffitt explained.

The elephant and the store it keeps safe from ivory hunters
are located at 3352 South Highway 191. There's no need to
make an appointment because the elephant stands guard 24
hours a day, so it's not going anywhere.

PLAYING THE LAST TUNE
San Carlos

The Apache violin and tequila have a couple of things in common—both are extracted from members of the agave family and, if not handled properly, both can give you a really bad headache.

Apache violins are crafted from sections of the stalk of the century plant, an agave that pops out of the ground, grows for about seventeen years, and then sends a huge shoot out of its

Terrill Goseyun, one of the last Apache violinmakers,
crafts the instruments from the stem of the agave plant.

center. Once the shoot blossoms, the entire plant dies. The violinmakers harvest the stalks, hollow them out, carve some holes, and string them with strands of hair from a horse's tail. They then make bows from sticks and horsehair and rub them with pine pitch.

Terrill Goseyun is one of the last Apache violinmakers. His grandfather, George Goseyun, was skilled in the craft and passed his knowledge down through the family. "I believe this form of art is facing extinction," the younger Goseyun said. "There are less than a handful of us in the Apache Nation that still practice it." So he divides his time in his studio here between making violins and creating intricate pencil sketches of tribal members. The violins sell for $200 to $600; his drawings command prices up to $16,000.

When played by an expert, the violins produce a distant, raspy wail. But in the hands of a novice, the sound is more like dragging a chair across a cement floor. Sort of like the noise your head makes after an extended encounter with tequila.

For details, check out www.apacheimages.com, or call (928) 475-6094.

S H R I N E   T O   A   F A L L E N   D O V E
What Used to Be Pinal

Mattie Earp was one of those historical footnotes, gone and almost forgotten except for an occasional reference when the Gunfight at the OK Corral comes up for discussion.

Her given name was Celia Blaylock, but she was known as Mattie, Wyatt Earp's first wife, although historians say it may have been a common-law arrangement rather than a legal marriage. But the famous Tombstone lawman dumped her to take up with actress Josephine Marcus, and the couple moved to

California after the shoot-out. Mattie, already a slave to the opium-laced elixir laudanum, hung around Tombstone for a while, then moved on to Pinal, a boomtown that sprang up around the rich Silver King Mine. Distraught over the breakup of her relationship with the marshal, she found solace in the bottle and died in 1888 at the age of thirty-one.

She was buried in a plot of ground set aside as a cemetery for deceased Silver King employees. Her grave was marked but relatively unnoticed until she became a matter of importance for Manny Guzman III of Superior, who knew about her final resting place because some of his ancestors are buried in the same plot. As an Eagle Scout project, he built a shrine at her gravesite. It's made of railroad ties and wrought iron, and there's a poem dedicated to her memory across the front. The inscription reads CELIA BLAYLOCK EARP, 1857–1888. Vandals damaged the original shrine, but Guzman repaired it.

Pinal is also just a memory, no longer on the map. The cemetery is on Silver King Mine Road off U.S. 60 west of downtown Superior. When the road forks, take the left one. It's only about 1.5 miles off the main road, but it's a tough 1.5 miles so a local guide and a four-wheel-drive vehicle are highly recommended.

A Town Goes Batty
Solomon

Not all the bats have flown from Solomon, but enough of them have that the school can stay open without fear of being battered. For years, the staff and students at Solomon School were forced to live with the winged creatures because, quite frankly, they couldn't get rid of them.

Every year, thousands of bats made an annual pilgrimage to the school, taking up residency in the attic. Since most school attics don't provide the basic necessities of life, the bat droppings up there could reach a depth of 6 inches after an invasion.

School officials hired exterminators and tried to seal off the openings with foam and wire. They erected bat houses in the hope that the critters would move in and leave the school alone. It worked but wasn't a solution. Once the bats realized how good they were being treated, they sent word back home and more bats showed up. This caused a housing shortage, so the newcomers had to take up residency in the school attic.

The sheer numbers rendered the school courtyard unusable for any activity other than dashing from classroom to classroom. Fortunately, nobody ever got bat bit.

Finally, after years of trying, the school contacted an international bat-removal agency whose workers used netting to trap the furry fliers and transport them to another area. Then they sealed the attic to prevent future intrusions.

But they didn't get all of them. Some of those who stayed moved across the road into a church; another flock relocated in a museum in Thatcher, about 20 miles away. Stay tuned. The hatches remained battened down, and this battle is still going on.

No Help for "The Helping Hand"
Superior

The town square here isn't very big. In fact it's more of a triangle than a square, and a small one at that. So small that if it weren't for the statue, there's a good chance nobody would notice it. But the statue gives it purpose.

It's called "The Helping Hand," and depicts a man reaching down to help a friend. It was hewn from a fifteen-ton chunk of dacite by a reluctant sculptor named Tom Macias.

It was a spur-of-the-moment thing, Macias says now. Back in 1982 the Superior Beautification Committee was tossing around ideas for the community's centennial celebration. "A friend volunteered me," Macias says. "He says, 'Tom, why don't you do a sculpture?' And before I could refuse, I was involved."

Macias had taken a couple of college art classes but had no formal training. There was also the problem of finding the right rock. If it was big enough, Macias couldn't handle it. A geologist found one out in the wilderness and the Kennicott mining company sent a flatbed in after it, then delivered it to Macias. "A bunch of guys came over and kind of horsed around," he says. "We all had our pictures taken, holding hammers and hard hats. But then they all left and I was all by myself with a fifteen-ton rock and no tools."

The rock was lying flat so he had to get a front-end loader to stand it up. His tool inventory consisted of a small hammer and a couple of chisels. And the dedication ceremony was seventy-five days away. Little by little the sculptor acquired the necessary equipment and skill to complete the project, but it was close. At midnight on the eve of the dedication, Macias was still putting on—or taking off—the finishing touches.

Macias is still a part-time artist, but he hasn't tried anything monumental since.

The sculpture sits on the town's main street, just north of U.S. 60.

WHERE MINIMALISM IS BIG
Superior

Even though it never gets any bigger, the World's Smallest Museum continues to be a work in progress. Owner Dan Wight doesn't add much to the museum itself, but he works constantly to improve the grounds that surround it.

Among his latest additions are two fountains. One is composed of used tires; the other is constructed of old mining equipment. The tire fountain features water drizzling down over a series of normal vehicle tires and pooling into a basin inside an eight-ton tire from a copper-mine truck. The miner fountain uses four old wheelbarrows to distribute the water as it falls.

The museum, a mere 128 square feet of working space, is subdivided into ten display areas, each with a separate theme. Each display is about 3 feet across, 2 feet deep, and 6 feet tall. This cuts down on crowds because there's room for only two people in the museum at one time.

The focal point is the roof, which Wight claims is the world's largest roof built of empty beer cans. "It took 1,800 empties to finish the job," he said, "but my selection committee did themselves real proud. They furnished 3,600 cans. Some of them are still recovering."

The museum, located in the Buckboard City complex on U.S. 60 on the west edge of Superior, is open daily. For details, try www.WorldsSmallestMuseum.com or call (520) 689–5800.

THE LEGACY OF THE BOOJUMS
Superior

Those unfortunate people who have nightmares about being chased by giant parsnips would do well to stay away from the boojum trees. Fortunately, they are quite rare and, according to most horticulturists, do not move well over land. So there's a pretty good chance nobody will ever be chased by one.

But for those who ate their parsnips as children and therefore have nothing to fear, a visit to a boojum tree can be a pleasant experience, because boojum trees are weird. They resemble a parsnip or green carrot sticking upside down out of the ground. It's a relative of the ocotillo plant, which grows wild all over Arizona, and the name comes from the mythical Boojum featured in Lewis Carroll's book *The Hunting of the Snark*.

According to boojum legends, when botanist/explorer Godfrey Sykes saw one in Mexico toward the end of the nineteenth century, he declared it looked like what a boojum tree should look like, so he gave it the name.

One place to find them is at the Boyce Thompson Arboretum, founded in the 1920s by mining magnate Col. William Boyce Thompson. It covers 323 acres and is home to more than 3,000 species of desert plants from all over the world.

The boojum trees are native to only two sites, both in Mexico. Those at the arboretum were transported from Mexico and transplanted shortly after the facility opened. They now stand well above 40 feet tall.

The arboretum is 3 miles west of Superior on U.S. 60. It's open daily except Christmas, from 8:00 A.M. to 5:00 P.M. And don't be afraid. The boojum trees have been desnarked, so they're harmless.

REEL VS. REAL
Tombstone

Although the actual incident occurred more than a century and a score of years ago, the controversy over the Gunfight at the OK Corral rages on. A few details are firmly established. It happened on October 26, 1881. The Earps and Doc Holliday were on one side, the Clantons and McLaurys on the other. Both sides glowered. Shots rang out. Two McLaurys and one Clanton died of gunshot wounds. Everything else is subject to interpretation and speculation that rage on to this day.

And one of the most hotly debated items is this: Was Henry Fonda a better Wyatt Earp than Kevin Costner?

Over the years the shoot-out has become a favorite subject in Hollywood. Earp has been portrayed by such major stars as Fonda, Costner, James Garner, Hugh O'Brian, Guy Madison, Randolph Scott, Richard Dix, James Stewart, Burt Lancaster, Joel McCrea, and Kurt Russell. And by a few whose names don't light up the memory banks, such as Harris Yulin, Buster Crabbe, Will Geer, James Millican, Bruce Cowling, and Bill Camfield.

An area in the Tombstone Courthouse State Historic Park dedicates space to the subject and even tries to give a factual account of what happened. Through drawings and verbal accounts the display attempts to retrace the episode from its start to its finish half a minute later. But even that attempt is flawed, because two versions are presented and the museum admits there could be errors in both.

The museum also has an exhibit about all the movies made in, and about, Tombstone. It's much more interesting. Especially the posters that show a young Jane Russell.

The courthouse is at 219 Toughnut Street.

A ROSE IS A ROSE IS A WHOPPER
Tombstone

Wyatt Earp's dead and buried. So's old Ike Clanton and his boys. Boot Hill is filled with those who lived and died in Tombstone, the place often called "the town too tough to die." About the only living thing that keeps on going ain't a gunslinger or a frontier marshal. It's a rose bush.

*The world's largest
rose bush covers
more than 8,000
square feet, which is
a substantial portion
of downtown
Tombstone.*

The Lady Banksia Rose is huge to the point of being awesome. The trunk is at least 4 feet in diameter and 8 feet tall. The arms cover a trellis system installed across a huge courtyard, spreading over an estimated 8,000 square feet.

Both the *Guinness Book of Records* and *Ripley's Believe It Or Not* list the rose bush as the world's largest. The locals say the claims have never been challenged, which is logical because rose experts don't normally go up against the Tombstone quick draws.

Amelia Adamson, who ran a boardinghouse for a mining company, planted the bush in 1885. The trellis was installed around 1904. The plant achieved international recognition in the 1930s when Robert Ripley proclaimed it the world's largest in his "Believe It Or Not" column.

The old boardinghouse became a museum in 1964 and is filled with antiques, artifacts, and memorabilia. And one humongous rose bush.

It's located in downtown Tombstone, just off Allen Street. For details, call (520) 457–3326.

THE JOY OF SADNESS
Tombstone

Gunfighters wearing their hats with the brims slouched low over the eyebrows are common here. So are woman dressed in 1880s' big hats and bustles. But those types surrender their rights to the main thoroughfare every year in mid-November when the clowns take over.

This happens during Emmett Kelly Jr. Days, an annual gathering of fat noses and crazy costumes held on the weekend closest to November 13, Kelly's birth date. The clown of world renown moved here in 1980 after a lengthy career as a circus performer. Although he turned seventy-eight in 2002, Kelly still dons the makeup and tattered clothing that transforms him into Weary Willie, the sad-faced character originally made famous by his father, Emmett Kelly Sr. But now the clown just goes by Willie to reduce the chance of mistaken identity, which is quite possible among a convention of persons going by such names as Lollipop, Bubblegum, Shoofly, and Tickles.

About thirty clowns from across the country take part in the event. They conduct clown seminars to answer such perplexing questions as, "Why don't clowns eat olives?" ("Because they can't get their heads in the jars.") They also march in a parade and participate in an auction that raises money for Tombstone high-school students. One year Kelly's dinner plate and a half-eaten roll sold for $79.

Fiddledeedee and Buttercup wanna-bes interested in more information should call the Tombstone Chamber of Commerce at (520) 457–9317.

Brother, Can You Spare a Buck?
Tortilla Flat

Tourists come to this tiny hamlet (population six) determined to leave money behind. They can do so in a variety of ways—buy souvenirs, have a beer, eat dinner, or pin a $1.00 bill to the wall. An amazing number select that last option.

Tortilla Flat, a stopping-off spot for centuries, was first used by the Salado Indians, later by a stagecoach line, and eventually by about one hundred families who took up residency. A flood destroyed the encampment in the 1940s, and it was never rebuilt. Now it's a tourist attraction featuring a general store, post office, the ubiquitous gift shop, and the Superstition Saloon.

The saloon decor is paper money, mostly $1.00 bills. They cover the walls, the ceiling, and the pillars that hold the building up. Most are autographed; others are stapled to business cards. Several bills are from foreign countries. Some visitors write checks; the amounts range from $1.00 to $1 million. According to old-timers, the custom started years ago when a merchant asked permission to put a business card on a wall. The owner at the time, so the legend goes, gave his okay if the card was accompanied by a dollar.

The practice has become so popular that when the restaurant burned to the ground in 1987, hundreds of former patrons sent new $1.00 bills to replace those lost. Now there are so many on display that they have become a tourist attraction unto themselves.

"People just want to be a part of Tortilla Flat," explained Lois Potter-Sanders, a longtime employee.

Tortilla Flat is about 18 miles east of Apache Junction on the Apache Trail (State Route 88). Investors can get details about where to put their dollars by calling (480) 984–1776.

CONFUSION AMONGST THE HALLOWEENIES
Tonto Basin

Confusion is almost a way of life for those who inhabit this small community. Some examples:

Is the official name Tonto Basin or Punkin Center?

Is that the world's largest pumpkin or just another plastic challenger?

Why is a state-record fish from Wyoming hanging out in the wilds of Arizona?

The kind and gentle patrons of the Punkin Center Store, Restaurant and Bar are always willing to help sort out the confusion, provided there's proper incentive and enough of it to go around. They say the town is officially called Tonto Basin because that's the name on the post office. But within the city limits (about 5 square blocks) there's another half-square block that is officially or unofficially (depending upon how much incentive has been flowing) known as Punkin Center, and that argument gets support because that's how it appears on most Arizona maps. So that point is still under study, incentive by incentive.

What may or may not be the world's largest pumpkin is also the sign for the Punkin Center Store, Restaurant and Bar. It's a plastic globe that measures about 6 feet in diameter and lights up at night. Francine Favazzo, who owns the establishment with her husband, Frank, said it probably is the world's largest but admitted she hasn't researched the claim on the Internet. It is, she said, most definitely the largest pumpkin in Punkin Center, a declaration that brings rousing cheers and demands for another round of incentives from her clientele.

As for the fish, it's a 23-pound rainbow trout that Frank Favazzo took from Burnt Lake in Wyoming back in 1969. It's still a state record for Wyoming. Rather than serve it to those who might forget the importance of his feat shortly thereafter, Favazzo had it mounted. When the couple moved to Arizona in 1979, they brought it along. When they bought the store/restaurant/bar in 2000, they hung it over the bar because it's a good incentive for more incentives.

Fishermen, incentive seekers, liars, and descendants of Ichabod Crane will find both Tonto Basin and Punkin Center on State Route 188, 13 miles to the southeast off State Route 87 between Sunflower and Rye.

S HRINE TO THE U NFAITHFUL
T u c s o n

J ust blocks from the heart of the city, a small adobe wall recalls a tragic love affair and betrayal. It sits on a small plot of ground next to a Mexican restaurant, and it's called either "El Tiradito" or "Wishing Shrine."

There are several stories about its origins, but the most popular involves an ill-fated love affair between Juan Olivera and his mother-in-law. When caught in an amorous act by his father-in-law, Juan was killed on the spot in 1880. But because he had sinned against his family and society in general, he could not be laid to rest in consecrated ground. So he was buried where he fell. Friends and relatives lit candles on the spot and prayed for his redemption. Over the years it became a shrine for parents worried about errant daughters.

Later the faithful adopted a custom that anyone could light a candle and make a wish, and if the candle burned to its base or burned through the night, the wish would be granted. That practice continues, and the site is now blackened from all the candle smoke and wax.

El Tiradito, perhaps the only shrine in the world dedicated to a sinner, is listed on the National Register of Historic Places. It's located on Main Avenue between Cushing and Simpson Streets, just south of the Tucson Convention Center.

RATTLIN' OVER BROADWAY
Tucson

The Diamondback Bridge can probably lay claim to several titles, like "the world's largest rattlesnake," "the world's longest rattlesnake," and even "the world's most artistic use of steel floor grating."

The pedestrian bridge—300 feet long, 16 feet high, and 16 feet across—spans Broadway Road, a major traffic arterial. It's the creation of Tucson artist Simon Donovan, who observed, "the proportions of the bridge seemed to be perfect for depicting a large snake." And so he made one.

Donovan selected steel floor grating and had it rolled into vaulted form to make the snake's body. When it came time to paint it, he created giant templates from huge sheets of rubber koi pond liner and attached them to the form with masking tape. "It looked like Lilliputians tying Gulliver down," Donovan said.

What's the better choice—walking through the belly of a
snake or walking across rush-hour traffic? Tucson
pedestrians get to make the choice daily.

Pedestrians can enter through either end. The mouth is fully
agape and supported by two iron beams that look suspiciously
like fangs, and the fiberglass eyes light up at night. At the
other end there's a giant rattle pointing skyward, and an electronic eye catches the movement of pedestrians and sets off the
sound of a rattle.

The snake's mouth is in Iron Horse Park at First Avenue and
Tenth Street. Don't be afraid to use it. But on the other hand, don't
go through it while you're singing "Fangs For The Memories."

NASTY LI'L FELLERS

*A*lthough *the rattlesnakes get most of the media attention, Arizona is also home to several other desert
denizens that can put the big hurt on those stupid enough to
stumble across one.*

*Male Colorado River toads are one example. Some of
them are big enough to fill a small cooking pot, but don't
try it, even if you're hungry enough to even consider making
one a meal. The toad can secrete a milky white substance
from the warts on its neck, and the fluid contains a toxin
that can kill a dog, even if only a small portion is ingested.*

*Back in the mid-1980s, a rumor spread through the
alternative lifestyle circuit that licking the back of a Colorado River toad offered a pretty good high. Several people
claimed they tried it without getting sick. But, according to
one anonymous source, they did get warts on their tongues.*

*There's also the Gila monster, one of two venomous
lizards in the world. Usually black and pink (or coral) colored, a Gila monster can grow to be 20 inches long. They are
shy, slow, and torpid, so about the only way to get hurt by
one is to pick it up, let it chomp down on some exposed skin,
and then let it hang on long enough for the poison to enter
the bloodstream. Gila-monster bites are extremely rare, but
the venom is highly toxic.*

*One bit of Arizona folklore claims that a man was once
convicted of murder by Gila monster.
According to the legend the victim
was in a drunken stupor when the
accused attached a Gila monster
to his hand and held it there while
it chewed in a fatal dose.*

SAYING "CHEESE" FOR POSTERITY
Tucson

Motorists making their first trips along east Broadway, one of the city's busiest streets, are literally exposed to culture shock because of the giant photographs that line a section of the road. They stand about 18 feet high and depict everyday scenes from the city's past.

The huge photomurals are the work of Tucson artist Stephen Farley, who called them "Windows to the Past, Gateway to the Future." They represent the bustle of a growing city, and they occupy major portions of four walls at an intersection. Using a process called "tilography," Farley transferred black-and-white photographs onto ceramic tiles and then embedded the tiles into the concrete walls.

The largest mural is 160 feet wide and is composed of fourteen photos of people walking, taken by street photographers more than fifty years ago.

The display is at the intersection of Broadway and Aviation. But drive carefully. Modern technology and speed cameras could be gathering photos for another wall sometime in the future.

AROUND THE WORLD IN FORTY WINKS
Tucson

The SunCatcher Bed and Breakfast is a rather worldly place. Although located in the Sonoran Desert, it can transport its guests to the Great Lakes, Asia, and Great Britain in moments, because each of the establishment's four rooms is decorated to imitate suites in world-renowned hotels.

This all came about in the early 1990s when globe-trotting Tucson attorney David Williams decided to bring memories of his travels home in a big way. He bought a house on Tucson's east side, remodeled the bedrooms, and converted it into a B&B. One bedroom is patterned after the Connaught in London; the others resemble lodging in the Oriental in Bangkok, the Regent in Hong Kong, and the Four Seasons in Chicago. But lest the guests get homesick, the lobby and dining areas are strictly Arizona.

J. C. and Carleen Carlson now own the inn, located at 105 North Avenida Javelina. For details on how to get there, call (877) 775–8355. And don't worry about winding up in China or Thailand. The Carlsons speak very good English, so their directions are easy to follow.

LOOKING AT ART AT 65 MPH
Tucson

The observation that one freeway overpass looks pretty much like the last one takes a direct hit when confronted with the Miracle Mile interchange along Interstate 10 in Tucson. It was one of the first major-freeway art projects in the state. It has spurred so many others that now the state's high-speed motorways are dotted with artistic renditions of lizards, kachinas, turtles, snakes, and critters of unknown backgrounds.

The Miracle Mile overpass features six large panels, created with ceramic tiles to represent the Southwest. The project was authorized by the State Department of Transportation and executed by Tucson artist Gary Mackender. Folk art, Mexican murals, and the colors and symbolism of modern Hispanic art inspired the panels. They're 35 feet wide, 9 to 20 feet high, and composed of 18,000 individual tiles.

The retaining walls holding the murals were cast in place, and then the tiles were attached. A fence incorporating a pueblo design on the walkway above the overpass completes the artwork.

The murals are on both sides of the overpass, so drivers can see them coming and going. But they have to look fast. It's freeway traffic, after all, and that usually means vehicles going 10 miles faster than the posted speed limit.

HISTORIC SPICINESS
Tumacacori

After the first step inside the Santa Cruz Chili and Spice Company, you know you're not in your average gift shop. The fragrance of the chili pepper permeates the small display area where more than 150 spices, powders, and chili-related concoctions are on sale.

With the exception of a small line of confectionery items and some cookbooks, spices are what's sold here. The lineup includes everything from chile de arbol powder to herbs de Provence to Vietnamese cinnamon. Some are mild, some are hot. Those uncertain about which degree of spiciness best suits their needs are invited to sample some of the wares at a table stocked with condiments. The sampling selections change daily. It may be some tongue-searing jalapeño mustard one day and sweet but spicy prickly pear jelly the next.

Gene and Judy England, who also owned the nearby Rock Corral Ranch, founded the company in 1942. A portion of the shop is devoted to a museum that traces the history of the ranch. There's no admission charge for getting a history lesson or inhaling some nasal-clearing chili powder.

Both the shop and the ranch are now owned and operated by
Jean England Neubauer, daughter of the founders, and her
husband, Bill.

The shop and all those wonderful aromas are at 1868 East
Frontage Road in Tumacacori, just south of and across the
road from the Tumacacori National Monument. For more information, call (520) 398–2591.

CREATING IN SOLITUDE
Turkey Creek

Turkey Creek and the dirt road named after it wind through
the woodlands at the base of the Chiricahua Mountains
with little intrusion by mankind. But then, shortly after the
sign on a fence points out that this is the El Coronado Ranch,
there's a small church, just sitting there by the roadside.

The Austins—Valer and Josiah—put it there. They own the
ranch. The 20-foot by 15-foot chapel is built of rock, and the
inside contains a small pulpit, some benches, and a wondrous
work of art that surrounds the interior. It is a fresco done by
Valer Austin and tells the story of the Creation. She devoted
five years to the project and had to travel to Mexico and Italy to
learn how to apply paint to wet plaster.

Once she acquired the knowledge and started the fresco, she
had to finish it in a hurry before the plaster dried. So she spent
eight consecutive days painting the walls.

The chapel is on private property, but it's okay to stop and
go in, even though it means parking your vehicle on a narrow
road and hoping an 18-wheeler doesn't come by. Enter through
a small iron gate and be sure to close it so the cattle don't get
out. And don't cross the footbridge leading to the ranch house.

To get there, take Turkey Creek Road east of State Route 181 for a little more than 7 miles. It's a well-maintained dirt road, but don't try it during or after heavy rains.

A CROSS-EYED HERO
Willcox

Most oater fans who watched Rex Allen fight the outlaws and rescue the heroines in the old B-Western movies never realized that he was once a cross-eyed country singer who performed at barn dances.

Fortunately for the millions who watched him save the Old West in the movies and on television, Allen had surgery to correct the defect shortly after his singing career took off in Chicago. But his eye problem is prominently mentioned on a bronze plaque placed next to his statue in Railroad Avenue Park here. The larger-than-life statue sits across the street from the Rex Allen Arizona Cowboy Museum and Willcox Cowboy Hall of Fame.

Allen was born in Willcox and got his start playing and singing with local bands before finding fame as a recording artist and singing cowboy. The community has been honoring him with Rex Allen Days since 1951. The museum opened in 1989, and Allen was a frequent visitor after retiring from show business. He died in 1999 and, at his request, his ashes were scattered around his sculpture.

There's also a small plaque in front of the statue honoring Koko, the horse Allen rode in his movies. A brochure for the museum says Koko is buried on the site.

Head-'em-off-at-the-pass fans can get more information by calling (877) 234–4111.

*A larger-than-life bronze sculpture of cowboy-movie star
Rex Allen stands guard over the spot where, some say, his
famous horse Koko is buried.*

THAT THING

The thing about The Thing is that once you see the thing you'll ask yourself why you paid a buck to see that thing. But The Thing is a billboard marketing success. A multitude of huge yellow road signs with blue letters advertise The Thing along Interstate 10 from Tucson to New Mexico. Sometimes they're solitary; other times as many as three pop up in a single mile.

Once at Bowlin's, a roadside stop near Willcox, travelers see the final sign, a huge yellow splash across the front of the building beckoning folks to see The Thing. Thousands do every year. They go inside, pay $1.00 and tour three tin sheds out back, where old cars, driftwood art, and other relics get the consumer prepped for The Thing.

It's in the third building under a smaller yellow sign. A glass-covered case holds what appear to be the mummified remains of an adult female and a baby. There is speculation that it's a fake, but others say it's real and should be given a decent burial. There have been several attempts to have it removed, but things like The Thing don't go away easily.

In case you miss the billboards, The Thing is at exit 322 off Interstate 10, about 5 miles west of Willcox.

HOW ABOUT A LITTLE DESSERT?
Willcox

Only the hungriest of the hungry should try to consume one of Corinne Stout's special homemade pies at one sitting. It may not be the biggest apple pie ever made, but it certainly goes beyond the average. And even if you've been apple pie–deprived since Prohibition, you're not going to finish one all at once.

The process begins when the pie maker pours ten pounds of raw apples into the peeler; when it's finished the creation fills a pie tin and stands about 10 inches high. Then it goes into the display at Stout's Cider Mill, where apple pie is not only an American icon but also a livelihood for Corinne Stout and her husband, Ron.

The mill opened for business in 1989. The couple planted their first orchard in 1985 and expanded to a second with 25,000 trees and 25 varieties of apples. That one got too big, so they downsized and began buying apples from other growers.

The vast majority of items on sale are made from apples. Besides the appetite-satisfying giant pie, they also bake and sell normal pies, apple cakes, apple cider, apple butter, and an applesicle that sells for $1.00.

Those in the market for a pie that'll feed the entire family, including that freeloading brother-in-law, will find the cider mill at 1510 North Circle 1 Road, just across the street from the Willcox Visitors Bureau. The Web site is www.cidermill. com; the phone number is (520) 384–3696.

TRIBUTE TO A FALLEN EARP

*T*he western movies never mention him, but there was another Earp sibling. His name was Warren and, unlike his three more famous brothers, he didn't survive his gunfight.

Warren Earp was killed in 1900 at the Headquarters Saloon in downtown Willcox. According to area historians, he worked on a local ranch and got into an altercation with Johnny Boyett, a cowhand with the same outfit. The story goes that Earp bullied his coworker into the shoot-out that ended in his death. When it was done, authorities discovered Earp wasn't carrying a gun, only a knife. But because Earp did have the knife in his hand at the time, Boyett was acquitted on the grounds that it was self-defense.

Wyatt and Virgil Earp allegedly showed up in Willcox a short time later, and Boyett mysteriously disappeared about the same time. Nobody here says the brothers had anything to do with it, but "Draw your own conclusions" is a common response to inquiries.

Although he never made it as a great historical figure, Warren Earp does have a legacy in Warren Earp Days, an annual convention for Western writers held in July. Also, a plaque commemorates the shooting at the former saloon (now a clothing store), and a welded steel marker has been erected at his gravesite in the Old Cemetery.

A L W A Y S   I N   T H E   F A M I L Y
W i n k e l m a n

The nice thing about Giorsetti's Grocery is that once you find it, you know it's always going to be in that same spot. At least it has been for almost a century.

Michele Giorsetti, an Italian immigrant, founded the little store around 1910. It was originally a bakery but gradually evolved into a mercantile that sold groceries and household items. The bakery is gone, but the current building is on the same site and, though the brands have changed names, the goods on sale are relatively unchanged. The elder Giorsetti died around 1950, and ownership of the store passed on to Provino Giorsetti, his son. When Provino Giorsetti died in 1993, his widow, Ruth Jean, and her sons Bill and Jeff took over.

Today it remains a common gathering place where residents of this old mining town meet to exchange greetings, buy supplies and, more than likely, share some gossip.

The store is at 307 Giffin Avenue, a block east of State Route 177 as it passes through town. Turn east at the post office and look for the wonderfully faded old sign on the side of the wonderfully old building.

Parker
Poston
95
Bouse
Quartzsite
95
Hope
10
Black Canyon City
17
71
Wickenburg
Aguila
60
60
Tonopah
10
Buckeye
85
Kofa National
Wildlife Refuge
Hyder
Gila Bend
Maricopa Ak-Chin
Indian Reservation
10
Gila River
Indian Community
Bapchule
347
84
Casa Grande
Arizona City
Dome
Yuma
8
8
95
85
Picacho Peak
State Park
10
Tohono O'odham
Indian Reservation
86
85
86
Sahuar
Arivaca
Amado
19

SOUTHWEST

SOUTHWEST

An Attic Filled with Ore Cars
Aguila

Sometimes, people start collecting things and pretty soon their collections get so big they have to put them in the attic or store them in the garage. That's sort of what happened to Charles and Jeri Robson, but on a massive scale.

They collected mining equipment, and their collection grew so large they had to build a whole town to keep it in.

It's not a real town. It doesn't have a mayor or post office or convenience store. But it does have a twenty-six-room hotel, a restaurant, and a gift shop. The place is called Robson's Mining World and it's clear out in the middle of nowhere, a patch of ground at the end of a dirt road 7 miles east of Aguila on Highway 71. There was a real gold mine on the site once, and some of the original buildings are still standing.

Charles Robson, who died in June 2002, claimed his collection was the largest of its kind anywhere in the world. It includes head frames, compressors, hoists, ore cars, stamp mills, flywheels, winches, drills, generators, and engines. It took 204 semi-truckloads to transfer everything to the site. The huge single-drum mine hoist had to be dismantled at its original location, hauled here on eight semis, and reassembled. Artifacts that size are major deterrents to shoplifting.

The hotel is cleverly disguised as Litsch's Boarding House. Although built in 1992, it looks old because the untreated wood exterior has weathered. Other buildings along the main street—the newspaper office, saloon, and general store—are only for show.

The museum is open October 1 through May 1. Hours are 10:00 A.M. to 4:00 P.M. weekdays and 8:00 A.M. to 6:00 P.M. weekends. There is an admission fee. For more information, call (928) 685-2609.

AN EAGLE'S-EYE VIEW
Ak-Chin Indian Reservation

There are times when becoming the world's largest something is an unattainable goal. That's why there are "second-biggest" categories, which makes a sculpture entitled *Desert Oasis* worth mentioning.

The piece is a 51-foot-tall bronze situated in front of Harrah's, a gaming casino that emerges from the desert on the Ak-Chin Reservation. It features a giant eagle getting ready to land on an even gianter saguaro cactus. Phoenix sculptor Snell Johnson masterminded the work and said it is the largest bronze sculpture in the Western Hemisphere.

Johnson also crafted the huge bronze lion that fronts the MGM Grand casino in Las Vegas. The eagle-on-cactus sculpture was cast in more than 250 pieces, then assembled and brought to the site on flatbed trucks.

There are varying opinions on whether or not it brings luck to those who patronize the gambling halls.

To reach the casino, ornithologists and fortune seekers should take Interstate 10 south of Phoenix to Queen Creek Road (exit 164), then drive south for about 17 miles. For more information, call (480) 802-5000.

A TOWN WITH BAD BREATH?

*I*f you come to Arizona, you're going to hear about Ajo. Not so much about the town, but how it got its name. "Ajo" is the Spanish word for "garlic." So it's only natural that most people, both the bilingual and the uninformed, assume the town was named after that ancient giver of the foul mouth, perhaps because it was a mining town and miners, as a rule, did not always smell good.

Some intellectuals, however, take it beyond such a simple explanation. The town, they say, was named after the ajo lily, a finicky desert plant that usually blooms in April. The edible root tastes like an onion, so the aftereffects are similar.

Both versions are colorful, but neither is true. Ajo in this case is actually a corruption of an old Indian word that means "paint." The area is laced with copper ore, and the O'odham Indians used copper to make a body paint they called "aau'auho." It was shortened and transposed into Spanish as "ajo," but it remains unclear how anybody could mistake "body paint" for "garlic."

Ajo, the town, is in Pima County on State Route 85, about 40 miles south of Gila Bend. And you don't have to hold your nose when you go there. It actually smells quite nice.

ONE BIG HUNK OF STEAK
Amado

There are some whose lives will not be complete until they have their picture taken while standing in the mouth of a huge cow skull. This fact alone makes a visit to the Longhorn Grill worthwhile; it's housed in a huge cow skull.

The skull is built of concrete blown over wire mesh and stands about 15 feet high. The horns extend 20 feet on each side, and the entrance to the grill is between what would be the nostrils if it were a live steer. According to local lore, it was

Eating lunch at the Longhorn Grill in Amado is sort of like looking at the cow from the inside.

erected as part of the scenery for the 1973 movie *Alice Doesn't Live Here Anymore* and has appeared in several other flicks, including *Boys on the Side*.

After the filmmakers left, the building/skull was converted into a bait and tackle shop. Since then it has also been a gift shop, bar, pizza place, and offices. It has been the Longhorn Grill since 1998. The restaurant is bright and airy, not at all like you'd expect the inside of a cow's head to be, and the walls are adorned with artistic renditions of the skull.

The place is located just west of Interstate 19 at exit 48. They serve steaks, burgers, and fries, but there's something a little unsettling about, well . . . you know . . . eating a steak inside a steer.

A *B* U M P Y   G O O S E
A r i v a c a

Arivaca's main street runs about 3 blocks long, and there's not much along the route to distinguish it from the primary thoroughfares of any other small town. The post office and saloon are on one side, the general store on the other, and the tire shop's down at the end.

But the community does have a goose sculpture, and it is a very lumpy goose. Created by the late Robert Friccione, it sits in front of the Main Street Artists Co-op Gallery and acts as the gallery's sign. Friccione, who was well-known in the area for the benches he made, used a large mesquite tree root as the creation's body. And because mesquite roots can be very bumpy, the goose is very bumpy. Except for the head and neck, which were carved from a mesquite plank.

The Arivaca Goose was sculpted from mesquite wood by Robert Friccione.

Since it's too heavy to move, the goose sits there rain or shine, day or night. You can honk when you drive by but don't expect a response. Bumpy gooses are rather aloof.

Arivaca is about 24 miles west of Amado off Interstate 19.

His House Rocks
Arizona City

Chuck Conway's house should withstand just about any-thing, including earthquakes, direct hits by mortar fire, typhoons, runaway 18-wheelers, and assaults by huffing-and-puffing wolves. The house is made of rock and weighs in at about 1,000 tons.

Constructing a rock house is relatively simple. First, get a whole bunch of rocks. Put the rocks into 3-foot wire cubes and stack the cubes on top of each other until they form a wall, leaving room for doors and windows. Next put in 4-inch steel pipes for bracing and spray the rocks with a concrete mixture. This gives the place stability.

Conway worked on the project for twelve years. To make sure it never falls down, he also bought old bridge timbers and used them as roof and ceiling beams. A fireplace and fans provide heat in the winter. To cool the house in the summer, when 115-degree afternoons are common, Conway dug a hole. It's 40 feet deep, 4 feet in diameter, and filled with rocks and 10-inch pipe. The air down there is a constant 50 degrees Fahrenheit, so it's drawn up through the pipes and forced into the house.

The floors are 3-inch handmade concrete tiles laid on a 16-inch concrete slab. The chopping block in the kitchen is an 11,000-pound hunk of marble. And there's a waterfall in the master bathroom.

"I'm sure glad it's done," Conway said after moving in during the summer of 2002. "But if I'd known it was going to take so long, I probably would never have started it."

The house is at 15553 South Yava, but it's not open for tours.

HIDDEN TREASURE OF A SPIRITUAL KIND

Bapchule

About half a century ago, Jimmy Stevens began applying paint to plaster walls in the little Indian mission churches spread across southern Arizona. Stevens, an Apache, married a Pima woman from the Gila River Reservation, and the couple moved to this small community about 40 miles south of Phoenix. He had displayed artistic talents in school and received permission from church and tribal authorities to paint large murals inside six churches on the reservation.

Jimmy enhanced the interiors of St. Francis Church at Ak-Chin, St. Peter's in Bapchule, the Holy Family Mission at Blackwater, Our Lady of Victory at Sacaton Flats, St. Francis Borgia at Sacate Village, and St. Augustine's Mission at Chuichu.

Stevens' best work is at St. Peter's, where he not only painted two murals but also decorated the ceilings and walls, combining Native American symbolism with Christian icons and turning the little house of worship into a mini–art gallery. Most of the other churches have fallen upon hard times, so Stevens' artwork crumbles with the walls. But St. Peter's is part of a mission school and is therefore kept in excellent shape.

To get there, take exit 175 off Interstate 10 south of Phoenix, go west on Casa Blanca Road for a couple of miles, and turn north at the St. Peter's sign.

TANKS FOR THE MEMORIES
Black Canyon City

Wesley Smith never planned to be an artist. It just happened. First he started collecting used 10,000-gallon gasoline storage tanks. Then his family bought him a new cutting torch.

Smith helped remove the old tanks from onetime gas stations and kept some of them on his property. But when local authorities told him the tanks had to go, Smith elected to recycle them as art. Using the cutting torch his wife and daughter gave him as a Father's Day present, Smith converted the tanks into huge sculptures.

The torch sliced through the quarter-inch-thick steel like a hot knife going through a chunk of butter, allowing Smith to carve intricate designs on an otherwise unworkable surface.

Wesley Smith used a cutting torch to turn discarded 10,000-gallon gasoline tanks into works of art.

A prime example of his craft stands at the Black Canyon City Community Library, a 25-footer entitled *The Story Teller* because the focal point is a cutout of a Native American figure.

Smith died in 1997, but his art is still prominent in the community. One piece is the marker over his gravesite. It's a 6-foot replication of the famous *End of the Trail* sculpture, cut from the end of an old gas tank.

TANKS BY THE ROAD
Bouse

Regardless of which way you're headed, State Route 72 enters and exits Bouse in less than five minutes. It would be easy to miss the whole town if it weren't for the enormous tanks sitting in a little park alongside the road.

There are two of them. Well, actually, there's only one—an M60 Patton. The other looks like a tank, but it's an M109 self-propelled howitzer. They look totally out of place on this barren piece of the Mohave Desert, but there was a time when tanks and other heavy equipment were common in the area. During World War II, Gen. George Patton selected several desert sites as training grounds for tank battalions.

Camp Bouse was located about 30 miles away from the town of Bouse, and it was one of twelve such installations erected in the deserts of California and Arizona. Six tank battalions, one armored infantry battalion, and an ordnance company trained at the site. Now the two war machines, seven concrete pillars adorned with plaques, and some murals pay homage to the time and the men who trained there.

Bouse is on State Route 72 between Parker and Vicksburg. The tanks are on the east side of the road. There's also a sign-in register in the park, asking for names of anyone associated with the units that trained here.

*The two old World War II war machines put drivers on
notice that they don't tolerate speeding in Bouse.*

THE HOBO WHO SURVIVED
Buckeye

When he was at the peak of his career, *Hobo Joe* stood tall
and beckoned the hungry to dine at a local eatery bear-
ing his name. He was one of several large figures that were
spread across the country back in the 1960s to advertise the
Hobo Joe chain.

But when the restaurant he symbolized went out of business, Hobo Joe was left destitute. Many of his fellow greeters were destroyed; this particular one soon became the object of scorn and the subject of a citywide controversy.

Marvin Ransdell, who also built the 25-foot fiberglass sculpture, owned the *Hobo Joe* statue in Buckeye. When Ransdell died, he willed it to Ramon Gillum, a close friend. Gillum asked that the work be resurrected in the downtown area, but his request met stiff local opposition. Some residents didn't want an oversized tramp as a symbol of their community.

Frustrated, Gillum decided to keep the statue for himself. After getting the necessary approval from the city, he moved *Hobo Joe* onto his own property, a meat-processing plant on the eastern outskirts of the city. It is one of only two such artworks left in the country, Gillum told city officials during all the commotion.

Now it rises on a pedestal at the east end of Monroe Street and extends a cheerful salute to all those who pass. A plaque at the base dedicates it to Ransdell's memory.

S *TEAKS* AND S *TICKERS*
C a s a   G r a n d e

Under most circumstances history and cacti are not compatible with steaks and burgers, particularly when it comes to dining out. But they go well together at BeDillon's, a restaurant where diners can undergo close encounters with prickly pears and saguaros while waiting for their chow.

The main building was erected in 1917 as a wedding gift for a young couple. They lived there until 1949, filling the surrounding garden with pointy plants from this country, Africa, South America, and Central America. The next owners built a small museum to display their collection of Southwestern historical and cultural items. It was still a residence when current owners Michael and Nancy Jackson bought the place in 1987 and converted it into a restaurant. But they left the cactus garden and museum intact and added new species and more stuff.

So patrons can stroll through the garden, examine newspaper clippings about Wyatt Earp and Cochise, try to identify what kind of cactus that is that just stuck them, and then go inside for dinner. And there's no need to worry about saving enough time and money for a trip to the gift shop. There isn't one; the only thing for sale is food.

BeDillon's sits on a corner at 800 North Park Avenue in downtown Casa Grande. For reservations, call (520) 836–2045. And be careful where you sit.

BASEBALL AT THE RESORT
Casa Grande

Today the Francisco Grande Resort is best known for its golf course, the longest PGA-sanctioned layout in Arizona. But the luxurious hotel can trace its ancestry directly back to baseball.

Located 5 miles west of downtown Casa Grande, the resort was developed in the early 1960s by Horace Stoneham, the then-owner of the San Francisco Giants, as a spring-training facility for his players. The 8-story structure boasts 112 rooms and suites and was surrounded by baseball fields, so housing and workout space for the team were more than adequate.

But Stoneham carried the baseball theme throughout the facility. The overhang on the main building was designed to resemble the brim of a baseball cap. The swimming pool is shaped like a bat, the wading pool like a ball. And the parking lot mimics the outline of a baseball diamond.

The swimming pool's shaped like a bat and the wading pool is a ball at baseball-oriented Francisco Grande Resort near Casa Grande.

The Giants left Casa Grande for Phoenix in the spring of 1970, and the practice fields disappeared shortly afterwards. But the baseball theme remains intact, and guests still swim in the pool where Willie Mays once cavorted. There's no dressing room at the pool, however. Stoneham apparently didn't want people asking for directions to "the batroom."

For more information, call (800) 237–4238, log on to www.franciscogrande.com or drive out to 26000 Gila Bend Highway.

THE SHIP OF THE DESERT
Casa Grande

There's something funny going on at the Triple C Furniture building. For one thing there's an anchor hanging off the front. For another there are portholes instead of windows along one side. In fact if you didn't know better, you'd say it looks like a boat.

A son in the navy was reason enough for a Casa Grande
merchant to erect a building shaped like a ship.

And you'd be right. It looks like a boat because it's supposed to look like a boat. From 1946 until 1981, the building housed an automobile agency operated by longtime Casa Grander C. J. "Blinky" Wilson. He built the structure to honor his son, Jay, who had served in the U.S. Navy during World War II. An inmate at the state prison at Florence designed the building, and it was christened the "SS Blinky Jr."

Original decorative features included tires imprinted with the building name hanging on the sides as life preservers, a Popeye character on the top, and a ship's bell from the Aleutian Islands. They're all gone now, but the name and the anchor and the portholes remain.

The building is at 511 West Second Street, a few blocks north of Florence Street.

COTTON ON CANVAS
Casa Grande

Carl Clapp's life and his art both revolve around cotton. Carl majored in art education in college and planned to teach art, but he shifted direction when his father-in-law urged him to get into cotton farming. The two were actually a pretty good matchup—Clapp could farm during the day and paint at night.

But it's his subject matter that sets him apart from other western artists. He paints cotton and only cotton. His acrylics depict the different stages of the cotton plant, from the time it blooms until the pods break open to reveal the white fluffiness inside.

"There were hundreds of western artists at the time, so I decided to paint what I know best," Clapp said, "and I know cotton."

His marketing strategy is also unusual. He doesn't show in galleries; instead, he sells through chemical, seed, and agricultural companies. This reduces advertising costs and overhead. Apparently it's working. His paintings are on display in offices and homes in America, Russia, France, England, Spain, Australia, and several Asian countries. A print of one of his cotton blossom paintings raised $30,000 for agricultural scholarships.

Clapp is semiretired as a cotton farmer, but his paintbrushes are still active. For more information, call him at (520) 836-2659. Be forewarned, however, that he's heard all the "see no weevil" jokes.

A WOMAN'S WORK?

S *even friends organized the Casa Grande Women's Club in 1913. Their first order of business was to raise money to put up a building so they could stop meeting in their own homes. Over the next decade the women formed a library, started a hot-lunch program for school children and, of course, tried to make enough money for their building.*

Plans for a Hopi Indian–style structure were drawn up in 1924, but the women still didn't have ample funds. So each member pledged to contribute something—a load of rock, bags of cement, wheelbarrows of sand, or the equivalent in cash.

To meet this commitment, several members went into the surrounding desert with horse and wagon and collected rocks. Not just any old rocks, however. They had to be feldstone, because that's what the plans called for.

The hard work paid off. The building was completed in 1925, and it's still a mainstay on historical tours of the community. The women continue to meet there but, faced with rising maintenance costs and declining membership, they deeded the building to the city in 1997.

It's located at the corner of Sacaton and Florence Streets. It'll be around for a while; the women found some extremely durable feldstone rocks.

TAJ MAHAL IN THE DESERT
Dome

Loren Pratt chuckled when asked if he's ever been compared to Shah Jahan. "No, but it's a nice thought," he said. "I truly loved my wife. This is in her memory."

For those who don't work crossword puzzles, Shah Jahan was a Mogul emperor who loved his wife so much that when she died, he had the Taj Mahal built in her memory. It was con-

This tiny shrine near Dome has a close connection to the Taj Mahal in India. Both were built for the love of a woman.

structed between 1632 and 1654 near Agra, India, as her mausoleum. Her name was Mumtaz-I-Mahal, and her monument stands nearly 330 feet tall at its highest points and features a massive double dome sitting atop a 260-foot pinnacle. An estimated 20,000 men worked on the building.

Pratt is a farmer and his tribute to his late wife, Lois, is not nearly so elegant. It is a tiny wooden chapel that sits on a flat spot in the middle of cotton and lettuce fields. The building stands about 15 feet tall and can seat six to eight people. With the help of friends and relatives, he constructed it in a few months in 1996.

The church is small on the outside and even smaller inside. The pews hold one person comfortably but can accommodate two if they don't mind sitting really close together. "Most visitors come in the winter," Pratt said. "In the summer they go inside and come out gasping and asking why there's no air-conditioning."

The chapel is located on U.S. 95 about 15 miles north of Yuma.

WELL, SNAKES ALIVE!
Gila River Indian Community

At first glance the Gila River Arts and Crafts Center looks like any other round building with something sticking up in the middle. But upon closer inspection, it sort of resembles a rattlesnake. And that's what it's supposed to be—a building shaped like a snake.

The design pays tribute to Snaketown, an excavation of old Hohokam ruins near the center. The village was first explored archaeologically in the mid-1930s, and it underwent extensive digging over a long period that began in 1964. The Hohokams are mysterious figures in Arizona history. They apparently moved into the area around the time of the birth of Christ and stayed until about A.D. 1100, when they up and left. Historians give many reasons for the departure, the most likely being extended drought. The site now is important enough to be declared a National Monument.

Erected in 1970, the center's exterior walls form a circle that sort of looks like a coiled rattler. The building is higher on one end, like a snake in a warning posture. A tower in the center is symbolic of the reptile's rattlers, adding to the effect. The facility contains a restaurant, a gift shop, and a splendid museum that traces the history of the Pima and Maricopa Tribes, the current inhabitants of the area.

The center is south of Phoenix on Interstate 10. Take exit 175 and go about half a mile west. Hours are from 8:00 A.M. to 5:00 P.M. daily except holidays. G'wan in. It ain't gonna bite ya.

WHERE THERE'S HOPE, THERE'S . . .
Hope

At first there was no Hope in Arizona. Then there was a little Hope. As the years went by, however, Hope was abandoned. But now Hope springs again.

Realistically there's still not much Hope. Although it appears on state maps, it's hardly a town. Only two houses, a gas station/convenience store, an antiques shop, and some mobile-home parks are within its boundaries. And during the summer months, the total population numbers fewer than ten. This pretty much negates the need for a police department, mayor, or domed football stadium.

But situated as it is at the junction of U.S. 60 and State Route 72, it's a convenient stopping-off place for motorists on their way to the Colorado River cities and California. And the gas station replaced one that burned down in the 1980s, so there is some hope for Hope.

Those who live there also have a good sense of humor, illustrated by the signs on the roads leading away from the community. They say, YOU ARE NOW BEYOND HOPE.

THE LONELY MONUMENTS
Hyder

There's a whole lot of "nothing but" out here. Nothing but sand and beer bottles. Nothing but heat and dust. Nothing but some old stone monuments. It wasn't always that way. Once, about sixty years ago, more than 40,000 men played war games here.

They were soldiers, and it was World War II. At the time of their arrival, France had been defeated, the British had lost the Balkans and Greece, and German troops under Gen. Erwin Rommel had joined up with their Italian allies in Egypt. In the United States, Gen. George Patton said he needed camps to prepare soldiers for action in North Africa.

Patton initially established desert-training facilities in the California desert. Within a year the operation was expanded to include two camps in the Arizona desert. Camp Horn was the home of the 81st Infantry Division; the 77th Infantry was stationed at Camp Hyder. The two were about 10 miles apart in the Sonoran Desert.

The operation was declared a success, but neither division made it to North Africa. The campaign ended before their training was finished. Both divisions were retrained and sent into action in the South Pacific.

Only stone pyramids mark the troops' presence in the Arizona desert. One stands about 15 feet high and bears the names of seven soldiers who died at Camp Horn. Two stone gateposts denote the entrance of what used to be Camp Hyder.

The sites are about 8 miles north of Interstate 8 off the Dateland exit.

WHERE THE WILD PALMS HIDE
Kofa National Wildlife Refuge

While this may be of interest to only a few, it's worth mentioning because nobody knows for certain how many wild-palm aficionados there are out there.

The Kofa National Wildlife Refuge is home to quail, desert bighorn sheep, desert mule deer, coyotes, bobcats, and others. Unfortunately for those who choose wildlife viewing as a hobby, all those creatures are shy and reclusive, making them hard to spot.

But what you can see are the wild palms. They're the only palms in Arizona that are native to the state. All those in the cities and along the roadsides are imports. Ironically, they're California fan palms, better known as "Washingtonia filifera" among the frond set. They've been in the canyon for decades, maybe even centuries.

Palmies, fronders, and others will find their quarry in Palm Canyon. To get there take the Kofa Refuge trailhead exit off State Route 95 about 62 miles north of Yuma and drive east for 7.5 miles to Palm Canyon Road. Then hike about half a mile to the canyon, where the palms are visible on the north side.

Use caution and common sense. Take plenty of water and watch your step. Some of the cliffs are steep and sprinkled with loose rock.

TUBE BE OR NOT TUBE BE
Parker

Tubing is a popular summer pastime on many rivers in Arizona. But the sport rises to extreme levels on the Colorado River during the annual Great Western Tube Float.

The event, held on the first weekend in June, draws Arizona and California tubes and tubers to the river, where they compete in a variety of competitions. The rules are pretty standard—all entries must be tube-based and no paddles, fins, or any other form of propellant are allowed. They just put 'em in the water and let the flow do the rest.

The float competition is the most fun. Designers can create anything they want as long as it incorporates inner tubes as the prime floatation device and, of course, as long as the craft stays above water long enough for the judges to inspect it. One float in the 2002 event consisted of twenty-one tubes tied together one behind the other. According to one observer, "it looked like a snake made out of licorice Lifesavers." Another prizewinner from the past was an outhouse mounted on inner tubes. It was called "The County Seat," because a bar of that name sponsored it.

The event marked its twenty-fifth anniversary in 2002. Between 650 and 900 tubers enter every year. For more information call the Parker Chamber of Commerce, (928) 669–2174.

THE WORLD'S DEEPEST
Parker

P arker Dam is one of several along the Colorado River, but it's the only one with a hidden distinction. It's the deepest dam in the world. The problem is, nobody ever sees that feature because most of the depth is underneath both land and water.

About 73 percent of the dam's structural height of 320 feet is below the original riverbed. During construction, 235 feet of the Colorado's bed had to be excavated before the concrete could be poured for the dam's foundation. Today only about 85 feet of the dam is above the riverbed, and less than that is visible because of the water levels.

The dam's superstructure rises 62 feet above the roadway. So it still makes a pretty good photograph, even if you can't see the bottom. And for those who need big numbers to impress the folks back home, the dam can impound 211 billion gallons of water.

Parker Dam is located 15 miles north of Parker on State Route 95.

THE REAL ROOSTER
Picacho Peak

T here really is a Rooster Cogburn. In fact, according to the Cogburn family, there have been Rooster Cogburns around for a long time and not just in the movies. One was even a U.S. Marshall back in Arkansas. There are Cogburns who say the

*There is a Rooster Cogburn, but he doesn't chase bad guys in
the movies; he raises ostriches near Picacho.*

character played by John Wayne in the movies is based on that
particular Cogburn.

You can find out about this and a whole lot more by stopping at Rooster Cogburn's Ostrich Ranch, where D. C. Cogburn
and his wife, Lucille, raise ostriches. Almost 2,000 of them,
with their heads sticking up over the fences looking for a
handout.

They're South African Black ostriches, and the Cogburns
claim they have the largest flock of them anywhere in the
world outside of South Africa. It'll probably stay that way,
Lucille said, because the birds haven't been allowed out of
Africa since 1948.

The Cogburns started ostrich farming in Oklahoma, but they moved to Arizona in 1993 because the climate is more conducive to bringing up longnecks. Although their focus is on raising birds for breeding, meat, and leather, the operation has also become a tourist attraction. So folks interested in things ostrichian purchase feed for $2.00 a cup and give it to the birds by hand.

And about that Rooster thing: Lucille Cogburn said all males in the family are nicknamed Rooster because the Cogburn family crest contains three rooster feathers.

The ranch is about a mile south of Picacho Peak. Turn your ostrichmobile off Interstate 10 at exit 219 and follow the signs.

PEAK-A-ROO-ROO

Mystery surrounds Picacho Peak, an old lava plug that has become a landmark between Phoenix and Tucson. The name, for example. Picacho Peak is a redundancy because "picacho" means "peak" in Spanish. Literally translated into English, "Picacho Peak" means "Peak Peak." Or, for the bi-lingualists, "Picacho Picacho."

Linguists and translators can ponder this matter by taking exit 219 off Interstate 10 about 30 miles north of Tucson.

COWBOYS AND REBS
Picacho Peak State Park

R hett Butler and Scarlet O'Hara never got this far west, but there were Civil War battles fought in Arizona.

The most significant one took place on April 15, 1862, when an advance detachment of Union forces from California attacked a Confederate scouting party. The battle raged for about an hour and a half. Three Union soldiers were killed, and three Confederates were captured.

The event is remembered every March at Picacho Peak State Park. More than 200 Civil War reenactors converge on the little mountain to re-create mock battles that took place in Arizona and New Mexico. Various monuments now pay tribute to both sides as well as those who died.

The state park, dedicated in 1968, covers 3,502 acres. It's just off Interstate 10 at exit 219, 40 miles north of Tucson. There are entrance and camping fees. Yankees, Rebs, and history buffs looking for more information should contact Arizona State Parks at www.pr.state.az.us, or call (800) 285–3703.

A MONUMENT TO SHAME
Poston

T he Colorado River Indian tribes erected the Poston Memorial Monument and Kiosk in memory of an injustice.

At the outbreak of World War II, 120,000 people of Japanese descent living on the West Coast and in western Arizona were removed from their homes under the provision of Executive Order 9066. They were relocated in ten internment camps in Arizona, Arkansas, California, Colorado, Idaho, Utah, and Wyoming.

The Poston monument marks the site of the Colorado River War Relocation Center, where a combined total of 17,867 men, women, and children were interned in three camps from May 5, 1942, to November 28, 1945. The single concrete column symbolizes unity of spirit and stands 30 feet tall. It was built as a cooperative effort between members of the Colorado Indian tribes and the Japanese community.

The inscription reads: THIS MEMORIAL IS DEDICATED TO ALL THOSE MEN, WOMEN AND CHILDREN WHO SUFFERED COUNTLESS HARD-SHIPS AND INDIGNITIES AT THE HANDS OF A NATION MISGUIDED BY WARTIME HYSTERIA, RACIAL PREJUDICE AND FEAR. MAY IT SERVE AS A CONSTANT REMINDER OF OUR PAST SO THAT AMERICANS IN THE FUTURE WILL NEVER AGAIN BE DENIED THEIR CONSTITUTIONAL RIGHTS AND MAY REMEMBRANCE OF THAT EXPERIENCE SERVE TO ADVANCE THE EVOLU-TION OF THE HUMAN SPIRIT.

It's not hard to find because there's not much else in Poston, which is located on the Colorado River Indian Reservation 15 miles southwest of Parker.

THE LEGEND BEHIND CAMELMANIA
Quartzsite

This community's most famous citizen is shrouded in mystery. Nobody knows for certain where he was born, when he was born, or what he was named after he was born. He died in 1902 but everyone who lives here knows who he was, and his tombstone is the biggest monument in town.

He went by Hadji Ali, Hi Jolly, and Philip Tedro. He was a camel driver, one of the first ever to be employed by the U.S. Army. As near as anyone can determine, he was born in Syria around 1828. His given name has been lost in history; he became Hadji Ali after converting to Islam as a youth. Whatever his name was, he came to the United States in 1856 when the army determined that camels could solve its transport problems in the arid Southwest.

Soldiers changed his name to Hi Jolly because they said it was easier to pronounce and remember. When the camel experiment flopped, Hi Jolly bought some of the camels and opened a freight line that operated along the Colorado River. He became a U.S. citizen in 1880 and used the name Philip Tedro on his papers. Tedro later married and had two children, but he abandoned the family and went prospecting for gold.

He died in an old cabin near Quartzsite in 1902; his memory lives on. His tombstone—a rock pyramid topped by a copper camel—draws thousands of visitors every year.

THE CAMELS COMETH
Quartzsite

Hi Jolly (or whatever his name was) is also the direct cause of camelmania, a rare but harmless malady that descends upon Quartzsite every year in the form of Hi Jolly Daze. It features contests for fiddlers and singers, but no camel-calling events.

The camel theme is carried out in other ways. At the Main Event, a longtime flea-market site, Howard Armstrong proudly displays a camel sculpture composed of motor-vehicle parts. Armstrong commissioned Oklahoma artist Jim Powers to create

Not all camels are made of skin, bone, and humps. This one, composed of old auto parts, sits on Howard Armstrong's property in Quartzsite.

the animal's body from tire rims, tie-rods, and transmission parts, while the head is a gas tank from a motorcycle.

Armstrong also purchased some turkey sculptures from the Oklahoman. "The tails are made from old tractor seats," he said. "They look really authentic." He keeps them in his home.

The Main Event and the automotive camel are on Quartzsite's main street just east of exit 17 off Interstate 10. For information on where to get your Hi Jollies, call the Quartzsite Chamber of Commerce, (928) 927–5600.

THAT'S ONE WELL-ARMED CACTUS

*F*olks in this area are a bit cautious about claiming any world records for their big saguaro cactus, so they add the phrase "possibly the world's largest" when explaining why the plant is worth a trip into the desert.

The cactus has forty-seven arms, possibly more. The "possibly" results from a reluctance among the locals to actually shin up the cactus to see if there are any more arms hidden under some of the larger ones. Saguaros, for the uninformed, have big unfriendly needles all over their bodies. The forty-seven arms that give the cactus its claim to fame also make it grotesque. They go left, right, up, down, crosswise, this way, that way, and over there. They also sag, droop, point skyward, and aim at the horizon.

Nobody knows the saguaro's exact age, but residents of nearby Quartzsite agree it's older than any of them. Saguaros can live for more than 200 years and don't grow their first arms until they're at least forty years old.

To see for yourself, get off Interstate 10 at the Dome Rock Road exit about 5 miles west of Quartzsite, then take Dome Rock Road east for slightly more than 3 miles. It's on the north side. There's a green sign that says GIANT 47-ARM CACTUS.

MOM-AND-POP RADIO
Quartzsite

Funny what people put in the spare bedroom. Take Maude and Buck Burdette, for example. They keep a radio station in theirs.

And it's not a ham-radio operation, either. It's KBUX, the voice of Quartzsite—the only radio station in town. It's a two-person operation, which makes programming quite simple: Put on some music and go do something else.

The daily format rarely changes. They play music most of the time, with brief interruptions for station identification and commercials. Not many commercials, however. They have only one regular advertiser in the summer and fewer than ten in the winter, when the snowbirds flock to the area.

KBUX is a 200-watt station with a range of 16 miles. Its primary listening area is Quartzsite and the huge chunks of desert surrounding the town. The signal occasionally reaches California, but that's not a big accomplishment because California is only 15 miles away.

The tower is a 70-foot telephone pole, and the promotions department is a vintage Volkswagen bug with a KBUX sign attached to the roof. They don't do ratings so they have no idea how many people are listening. But, as Maude said, "Pretty much everybody in town tunes in at one time or another."

The couple has more than 3,000 LPs stored in what used to be their living room. Buck transfers the music onto twenty-eight-hour reels so the station can stay on the air twenty-four hours a day without his having to tend to much. He also announces the selections, which range from old songs to big bands, gospel, ballads, a little light rock, and anything else they like.

To listen in when you're in the area, turn your dial to 94.3 FM, "the heartbeat of Quartzsite."

YOU WANT FRIES WITH YOUR HIGHWAYS?
Quartzsite

John Lintz has this thing for *Arizona Highways*, the popular magazine that touts the state's beauty through photographs and prose. He collected issues for many years and says the magazine was a major factor in his decision to relocate to Arizona in 1970.

And now that he's a full-time Arizonan and owner of a travel plaza in Quartzsite, he shares his devotion with those who pass by. He has decorated the plaza's Burger King in "early Highways." About twenty-five covers, both black-and-white and color, are displayed along the booths and on the walls, and a yellow stripe imitates a highway across the tile floor.

John Lintz put his extensive collection of Arizona Highways *memorabilia on display in his fast-food outlet in Quartzsite.*

A large neon-sign replica of Arizona's state flag hangs on a wall facing a montage composed of memorabilia and clippings from the magazine. And a large map of the state blasted into a chunk of sandstone sits outside the entryway.

The plaza is at the intersection of Interstate 10 and State Route 95 in Quartzsite.

THE TITAN THAT NEVER CLASHED
Sahuarita

The Titan Missile Museum isn't scary like a creaky old haunted house or an abandoned ghost town, but when you stop to consider the damage one of those things could have done, it goes way beyond frightening.

During the Cold War, several Titan missiles armed with nuclear warheads were planted in deep holes and aimed at the Soviet Union as a matter of defense. None were ever fired, so nobody knows for certain what the consequences would have been, which is just as well.

The Titan Missile Site, originally known as Site 571-7, was one of fifty-four sites in three states to be spared after the nuclear disarmament treaties were signed. There's still an actual missile there, but it has been disarmed. It was removed from the silo and left aboveground with holes cut into its re-entry apparatus and propellant tanks for thirty days to allow satellite observation.

Now the complex is a museum to something that never happened. Visitors take fifty-five steps down to the launch site 30 feet underground and watch a simulated countdown procedure. Then they get to poke around in an area originally designed to start or prevent a nuclear war.

To reach the museum, take exit 69 west off Interstate 19 and follow the signs. There's an admission charge. For more information, call (520) 625–7736. And don't go pushing any buttons. You never know.

NO NUDES IS NOT NECESSARILY
GOOD NEWS
Tonopah

Nudity is not encouraged at the El Dorado Hot Spring. But on the other hand, it's not discouraged, either. Lifetime partners Camilla Van Sickle and Bill Pennington frequently shed everything but their earrings and, since they're the owners, it's probably okay for their guests to do likewise.

"But if you're going to sensationalize nudity, you've come to the wrong place," Pennington cautioned. "It's a natural way of life." So, technically, El Dorado Hot Spring isn't a nudist colony. In Pennington's words, "It's a nice quiet place where people can come for a good soak."

There used to be seven hot springs in the Tonopah area; El Dorado is the only survivor. The spring is fed by an underground aquifer, and the water comes to the surface heavily laden with both heat and minerals. Guests can soak in a variety of tanks, ranging from a concrete enclosure built more than seventy years ago to steel tanks normally used to water livestock. Each soaking area is private, surrounded by lush vegetation that grows readily in the desert because the used water is recycled as irrigation through a series of canals.

And, although it's not a nudist colony, Pennington unashamedly pointed to a story about the place in *The World Guide to Nude Beaches and Resorts,* which he called "the bible of skinny-dipping."

Tonopah is 40 miles west of Phoenix at exit 94 off Interstate 10. A large sign on a water tank points the way to El Dorado. If you want to find out more about the bare facts, call (623) 386–5412.

DO THEY EVER PLAY THE TERRIBLE TOADS?

*T*he Salome High School athletic teams are probably the only athletes in the country nicknamed "the Fighting Frogs." This is a tribute to a legendary frog that couldn't swim.

The nonaquatic amphibian was the creation of Dick Wick Hall, a humorist and country philosopher who came to Salome early in the twentieth century, embarked upon a variety of get-rich schemes, and gave the community its name. His version was that a pretty young woman once removed her shoes on an inferno-like summer day and did an impromptu dance on the hot sand, so he called the place "Salome—Where She Danced." But history says he named it after the wife of a business partner.

The frog that couldn't do the breaststroke was among the creations Hall dreamed up for his stories, which appeared in national publications and the Salome Sun, a mimeographed sheet he published for distribution to travelers who stopped at his service station. According to Hall the frog was seven years old, and it couldn't swim because it had never seen rain or a pond. The unfortunate creature had to carry a canteen on its back to keep itself green, and he once chased a dust storm for miles because he thought it was a rain cloud.

Hall died in 1926. His grave is on Center Street, just down from the VFW Post 3708. But his frog lives on, at the high school and across the community. Frogs are prominent figures in local advertising, and frog statues are hot items among the tourists. There are very few real frogs in town, however. Salome gets less than 7 inches of rain per year, so it's no place for any self-respecting frog.

Frogs are big in Salome as both historical and tourist-oriented items. Randy Cervantes, a former student at Salome High School, poses with one of the school's "Fighting Frogs" mascots.

THE HISTORY OF THE BOLA
Wickenburg

The bola tie was proclaimed Arizona's official neckwear on April 22, 1971. Governor Jack Williams signed the bill, which made Arizona the only state in the union to have an official neckwear. The bill was defeated several times before being passed because lawmakers refused to take it seriously. One suggested that blue jeans be designated the state's official pants; another wanted to make the margarita the official drink.

It's only natural, however, that the bola be so honored. It was invented in Arizona during the late 1940s, when cowboy Vic Cedarstaff of Wickenburg hung a fancy silver-mounted hatband around his neck. A friend complimented him on his choice of neckwear and Cedarstaff, also a silversmith and leatherworker, transformed the hatband into a string of braided leather, tipped with silver globes and threaded through a silver and turquoise slide. Another friend said it looked like a South American bola, a device used by gauchos to catch cattle, and so the tie and the name came to life.

Northern Arizona University became the unofficial bola-tie capital of the world in 1996 by accepting a collection of almost 250 bolas from longtime Phoenix television newscaster Bill Close. Viewers sent them to Close in the hope that he'd wear them on the air. He claims he wore each one at least once, even though they included bolas made of golf balls, rattlesnakes, copper slag, eyeglasses, and elk droppings.

The university later donated the collection to the Desert Caballeros Museum in Wickenburg, which is open from 10:00 A.M. to 5:00 P.M. every day except Sunday, when it's open from noon to 4:00 P.M. Bola-tie enthusiasts can admire the neckwear for a $5.00 admission fee, but those age 60 and older (which most of them are) can come in for a mere $4.00. Don't display your non-Arizonaness by calling it a "bolo" tie. A bolo is a machete, used by some cultures to whack sugarcane, jungle growth, and, quite frequently, each other.

The museum is at 21 North Frontier Street. Neckwear aficionados in need of more information can call (928) 684–2272.

PINOCCHIO OF THE OLD WEST
Wickenburg

Jim Cook admits he sticks pretty close to the truth these days. "I'm happily married, don't drink, and I'm a recovering journalist so there's no reason to lie anymore," he said. This is almost heresy, coming from a man who bears the designation Official State Liar of Arizona.

"I read somewhere that the average person tells more than 200 lies a day," he chuckled. "I'm down to one or two a day, but when I tell one, it's a good one." Then he listed a couple of his favorites:

"When I was a kid, the trees in the Petrified Forest were still alive and the Painted Desert was just white sand with numbers on it."

And, "It was so hot my shadow got up off the ground and walked alongside me."

He appointed himself to the official liar position because the state didn't have one. "Besides," he said, "by doing it myself I don't have to kiss up to the governor to get re-appointed." Because an official liar needs an official raison d'être, Cook also created the Wickenburg Institute for Factual Diversity. From there he disseminates his Journal of Prevarication via electronic mail. It comes out about once a week, or whenever

As the state's official liar, Wickenburger Jim Cook deals only with the bear facts.

there's a need for a factually diversified anecdote. He has also published a book containing some of his better whoppers.

Cook worked on newspapers in Utah and Arizona for more than forty years before retiring to Wickenburg, where the climate is ideal for letting one's nose grow to great lengths.

Fibbers, half-truthists, falsifiers, prevaricators, and golfers in need of social understanding may contact Cook at azliar@aol.com.

FISHY TALES
W i c k e n b u r g

Like many other rivers in Arizona, the Hassayampa doesn't flow very often. Once a year if there's good rain, and then all the water comes in a hurry and doesn't stick around very long. The rest of the time, it's a sandy, dry streambed that bisects Wickenburg and slows out-of-state travelers, who gawk from their vehicles to see why it's called a river when there's not a drop of water in it.

But the Hassayampa serves purposes other than flowing and rippling. It is a thing of legend and falsehood, and it gives the locals something to lie about. For example, legend—and a sprinkling of fact—says there actually is a river there, but nobody can see it because it flows underground. In fact the name Hassayampa, as translated from an early Native American dialect, means "river that flows upside down."

Also, the locals say anyone who drinks the water from the Hassayampa (on those rare occasions when it's on the surface) suffers a strange fate. The victim immediately becomes a Hassayamper and is rendered incapable of ever telling the truth from that day forward. The locals say this makes it very popular with politicians.

As part of the folklore surrounding this waterless waterway, the chamber of commerce got permission from the Department of Transportation to erect signs on the bridge over the river. They have been there since 1930; they read NO FISHING FROM BRIDGE.

Despite that, some local merchants offer fake fishing licenses, along with instructions on how to catch and cook sand whales and other denizens of the dunes.

Assuming there actually are fishermen who distort the truth, as so many old wives tales indicate, they can get more information about this type of angling by contacting the Wickenburg Chamber of Commerce at www.wickenburgchamber.com or calling (928) 684–5479.

BOTANICAL INCARCERATION
Wickenburg

The old mesquite tree stands right in the middle of downtown. It has been around longer than anyone living here can remember. Local historians say the tree has been growing in that location for more than 200 years, and they have scientific evidence to prove it.

They also say it used to serve as the community jail.

A sign next to the tree supports the claim. It says, FROM 1868 TO 1890, OUTLAWS WERE CHAINED TO THIS TREE FOR LACK OF A HOOSEGOW. ESCAPEES WERE UNKNOWN.

The venerable mesquite is about to be glorified for its years of service. Sometime during 2003 it will become the centerpiece of a new pedestrian walkway that will lead to the community center.

The tree is located at the corner of Highway 60 and Tegner Street.

THE GEEZER TRAIN
Yuma

If it's the size of the toy that counts the most, there's a gang of elderly youngsters here who should walk off with the blue ribbon. They own a train. A real train, not one of those scale models that runs around on a piece of plywood.

They call it the Yuma Valley Railway, and they officially call their organization the Yuma County Livesteamers. Unofficially, however, they refer to themselves as "some old geezers who like trains." They bought the train in the late 1980s. It can haul up to 250 tourists on a 34-mile trip along the Colorado River. Although their average age is "darn near eighty and some younger'n that," the owners are also the crew.

A few of the Livesteamers were actual railroaders, a necessity because federal laws require that an experienced engineer drive the train with another one on board in case of emergency. But many of the others gained their expertise operating model trains in their basement. Sam Bova, one of the darn-near-eighties, figures he makes about fifty trips a year. He sells tickets and snacks and acts as conductor.

The club owns four cars and a couple of engines. One of the cars is a 1923 Pullman coach that portrayed Judge Roy Bean's private car in the movie *The Life and Times of Judge Roy Bean,* starring Paul Newman.

The train runs Saturdays and Sundays from October 1 through June 30. They take the summer off because the cars aren't air-conditioned. The train moves along at 12 miles per hour, so each journey lasts about 3½ hours. When it pulls back into the station, Sam Bova helps the passengers unload and then, like a good railroader, walks along the train and kicks the tires to make sure everything's in working order.

For information, call (928) 783–3456.

IT'S BETTER THAN "THUGS"

The Yuma Territorial Prison was an infamous player in the drama of the Old West. For thirty-three years it served as a place of incarceration, and some of those who stayed within its walls were indeed desperate men and women with no redeeming qualities.

But many others wouldn't even be sentenced to prison today for the crimes they committed more than a century ago. From the time it opened in 1876 until it was shut down in 1909, it housed a total of 3,069 inmates convicted of everything from murder to polygamy to seduction. Few served their full sentences, however. Paroles and pardons were easy to come by in those days.

In 1910, a year after the prison closed, the local school district needed space for a high school, and they utilized the old lockup without making any major architectural changes. That relationship lasted until 1914, but the time in history is well preserved— Yuma High School's athletic teams are still nicknamed the Criminals.

The Criminals are now housed in their own high school, and the prison is now the Yuma Territorial Prison State Park, open daily from 8:00 A.M. to 5:00 P.M. with a nominal admission fee. James Cagney and George Raft fans can get more information by calling (928) 783–4771.

S TAYING A LOFT THE H ARD W AY
Yuma

An old airplane dubbed *The City of Yuma* has been painstakingly restored and given a permanent home here. It's an Aeronca Sedan AC15 that once helped the city get through a financial crisis by spending more than 1,000 consecutive hours airborne.

In 1949, while Yuma was suffering from a postwar economic depression, several businessmen decided that an endurance flight would put the community in the international spotlight. They got sponsors, volunteers, and donors to donate the plane, a refueling car, and their time, and then they set out to break the existing record. The plane had to be rigged to handle extra fuel and supplies and the refueling car, a 1949 Buick convertible, was outfitted with a platform on the back. The volunteers would stand on the platform and pass the necessities to the plane flying 3 feet overhead while both were roaring down the runway at more than 70 miles per hour.

The first two attempts failed due to trouble with the plane. But the project was finally launched successfully on August 24, 1949. Pilots Woody Jongeward and Bob Woodhouse took four-hour turns at the controls, then slept or made adjustments and repairs on the plane. They had to maneuver the aircraft over the Buick twice a day to make the exchanges. The fuel was handed up to the nonflying pilot in 2½-gallon cream cans, and the plane-to-car handoffs had to be exact or the vehicles would collide.

There was also the problem of going potty. Prior to the flight the ground crew furnished a small aluminum pot and some waterproof bags. Woodhouse said that "whenever you got whatever you wanted into that pot, then you'd pull it up and twist that little wire around the top (of the bag), and then we'd fly over to California and throw it out 'cause we had heard that they needed the water over there."

The pair stayed aloft until October 10. They flew 89,920 miles while establishing a world record of 1,124 hours (more than 47 days) before landing in front of 12,000-plus spectators. The stunt was covered by international news media and may have been instrumental in creating an economic upturn that followed. But their endurance record endured for less than ten years. Two Nevada pilots stayed aloft for more than sixty-four days from December 1958 to February 1959.

The *City of Yuma* was later sold and wound up in Minnesota. In the early 1990s the Yuma Jaycees spearheaded a project to buy it and return it to the scene of its former glory. Now restored, the plane is kept in the Betko-Air building at the Yuma Airport and is viewable during normal working hours. There is a move under way to put it on permanent display in a new visitor center planned for the downtown area. For details, log on to aztec.asu.edu/enduro49.

WATERED-DOWN ART
Yuma

Most communities adorn their water towers and tanks with either the name of the town or the first initial of the town's name. But Yuma opted for a triptych, a large mural that spreads across three huge tanks.

The city council received gallons of flak when it approved the $50,000 project in 1999, but the criticism died down a year later when the work received an award from the Governor's Pride in Arizona committee. It was designed and executed by Tucson artist Tim Merrick, who called the work *The Rio Project*.

The three tanks each hold three million gallons of water and handle about 50 percent of the city's water supply every day. They sit on a hilltop overlooking Interstate 8 and Sixteenth Street. And the city doesn't charge for looking at them.

WATCHING THE KNIGHTS FALL
Yuma Proving Grounds

P arachutist watching is a big winter sport here, and it's real easy on the wallet.

The Golden Knights, the U.S. Army's precision parachute teams, hold their winter jumping sessions at the Yuma Proving Grounds. The soaring soldiers go through a rigorous training schedule that begins in mid-January and runs through mid-March.

The Knights parachute onto grass-covered Cox Field, where bleacher seats are provided for those who get their thrills by watching men jump out of perfectly good airplanes. The teams jump continually from 8:00 A.M. to 4:00 P.M. Monday through Friday, and there's no admission fee.

The proving grounds, where the army also does extensive weapon and armament testing, are located off State Route 95 about 20 miles north of Yuma. Look for the big guns at the entrance; then drive about 4.5 miles west. Be sure you're not sitting around watching an empty sky; find out when the chutists are jumping by calling (928) 328–3394 ahead of time.

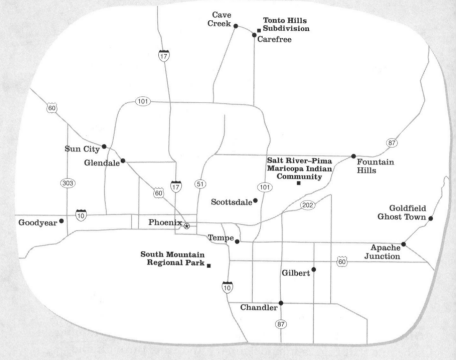

VALLEY OF THE SUN

VALLEY OF THE SUN

THE SNAKE HOLE GOLF AND COUNTRY CLUB
Apache Junction

There are about 190 golf courses listed for the metropolitan Phoenix area. The Snake Hole Golf and Country Club isn't on the list, however, because its members march to a different 5-iron.

It's not a long course—nine holes, par 29. The first hole is a tricky little 89-yarder that crosses creosote bushes, open desert, and the exact spot where one member says he saw a rattlesnake. Like all the others, the first green is small and brown because it's sand, not grass. This is not uncommon at Snake Hole. There's no grass. Anywhere.

The course sits on five acres of leased desert. Membership is restricted to residents of the Countryside RV Resort, located directly across the road so members don't have to put a lot of miles on their golf carts. Because the entire course is sand, there's no need for sand bunkers. No grass bunkers, either.

The greens are a darker shade of brown because they're oiled sand. This holds the putting surface down when the wind blows. The members are mostly winter visitors on limited budgets, so they're also the greens keepers. This means they have to find their own used oil. Some of it comes from fast-food restaurants, leading to the oft-asked question, "Would you like fries with that double bogey?"

Sand golfers also allow "stands." The ground is so hard they can't use regular tees even if they whack them with a driver, so they stand their ball on little three-legged plastic gizmos before hitting it. Another deviation is the rattlesnake rule. If you see a rattler, you get to pick up your ball and subtract as many strokes as you think necessary to get your heart rate back to normal.

The Snake Hole Golf and Country Club is on Idaho Road just north of the Superstition Freeway. Membership is $15 per year.

INSTANT RUINS
Apache Junction

In the words of Al Ferguson, "One of the largest structures on most properties is also the most boring. It's the concrete-block wall that surrounds it."

Ferguson, an artist, had looked at the dull gray surface in his backyard long enough to realize it wasn't going to look like anything other than a dull gray surface if he didn't do something to rectify the situation. And so he did. He turned it into *Greetaly*.

Using the same oil paints he normally applies to canvas, Ferguson turned his block fence into a mural that depicts the art and ruins of Greece and Italy, hence the name. The work includes the Parthenon, the Acropolis, and the Roman Coliseum. Since historical and geographic accuracy were not significant to the piece, he also included his renditions of the *Venus de Milo*, the *Discus Thrower*, and Michelangelo's *David*. The work is about 25 feet long and 6 feet tall.

"I can walk into my yard and I'm thousands of miles away and thousands of years back in time," Ferguson said. His wife,

Apache Junction artist Al Ferguson decided his block fence
was too bland, so he turned it into depictions of ancient
Greek and Italian ruins and named it Greetaly.

Vera, said she likes it "because I can look out my window and
there's David."

The mural isn't visible from the street, but the Fergusons
welcome visitors on weekdays from 9:00 A.M. to 2:00 P.M. They
live near Thunderbird Road and the Apache Trail in Apache
Junction. If you want to see where Greetalians and Italeeks
come from, call (480) 983–3573 for an appointment.

BUT WHEN IS IT MIDNIGHT?
Carefree

Whenever the conversation in Carefree turns to the subject of casting a giant shadow, the Palmer Sundial becomes a focal point. It is the largest sundial in the Western Hemisphere, measuring 62 feet long and 4 feet across and standing 35 feet above the desert floor, pointing to the North Star.

The huge teller of time was designed and executed in 1958 by solar-engineer John Yellot and architect Joe Wong for K. T.

The world's second-largest sundial in Carefree tells time and also produces solar energy.

Palmer, one of the cofounders of Carefree. The local Kiwanis Club took care of the sundial and surrounding park area for several years, then donated it to the city in 1988.

The dial casts its giant shadow on the twelve 3-foot concrete circles that surround it and mark the hours. A smaller sundial has been placed at the base of the big one, apparently as a backup. Neither functions well after sunset, however.

The sundial is not only a timepiece and tourist attraction but also a solar water heater that services a nearby office complex. Local lore says the dial is second in size only to astrological sundial observatories erected in India more than 250 years ago.

Located in Solar Plaza at Cave Creek Road and Sunshine Place in Carefree, the dial is surrounded by a small park that features a reflecting pool and waterfall. This makes it a very nice place to pass the time of day.

ONE TREMENDOUS HANGOVER
Cave Creek

The list of potables at the Satisfied Frog, a local watering hole, is strikingly different from those at other establishments. For example, the tap beers include "Juanderful Wheat," "South of the Border Porter," and "Big Horn Bock," all local products. They also brew and sell "Cave Creek Chili Beer," advertised as "the world's only beer with a chili pepper in every bottle."

But what they don't sell very much of is their house specialty—the $199 Margarita. As of winter 2002 the drink had been on the menu for more than nine months, but bartender Kathie Hobart said the saloon is still waiting for someone to walk in, plunk down $200 for a drink, and expect only $1.00

back in change. Although pricey by any standard, Hobart said the cost is justified because if they ever do make one, it'll contain two shots of a Selecion Suprema, tequila that has been aged in oak and sells for $75 an ounce.

It'll also contain hand-squeezed lime juice, Grand Marnier, and Mexican raw sugar, and it'll be served in a sixteen-ounce mug. If they ever do sell one.

So if it's not a big seller, why keep it on the menu?

"Well, you never know," Hobart replied. "Maybe someday . . ."

For oil barons, rock stars, and others interested in ingesting their alcohol at about $10 per gulp, the Satisfied Frog is at 6245 East Cave Creek Road. And for those who have one and like it so much they have another one for the road, there's a drug store with a good supply of aspirin right down the street.

HANG ON AND TURN LEFT
Chandler

Every year around the first or second weekend of March, grown men try to ride ostriches here as part of the city's annual Ostrich Festival. It's much easier to talk about riding an ostrich than to actually ride one, because nobody has yet developed an ostrich saddle. So riders have to get hold of something to hang on to. But ostrich necks are quite flexible, making them not very easy to hang on to. The recommended method, therefore, is to get on, grab a wing, and hope for the best.

This also is not easy. The feathers on an ostrich's back are slippery, and ostriches can run quite fast, some say up to 30 mph. Some of them stand 5 feet off the ground, so when a rider falls, it's usually a straight plunge downward, off the bird's rear end onto the rider's.

Other ostrich jockeys ride in little carts harnessed to the long-legged runners. That doesn't guarantee success, however. Ostriches are notoriously bad at following such commands as "Turn left!" and "Stop!" Especially "Stop!" This results in ostrich pileups and overturned carts, sort of like ratite rush hour.

The festival is held to commemorate the role ostriches played in Chandler's history. There were once thousands raised in the area when ostrich feathers were in big demand by the fashion industry.

But the ostrich festival became an ostrichless festival in 2003 due to an outbreak of Newcastle disease, an ailment that affects birds of all sizes. As a result, racing fans got to watch buffaloes, camels, and bulls compete. The birds are expected back in 2004.

For details on the races, the festival, and ostrich wagering, call the Chandler Chamber of Commerce, (480) 063–4571.

RUNNING WITH THE WEE ONES
Chandler

Chandler also has something for those who think ostrich racing is for the birds. It is the annual Running of the Chihuahua, that tiny breed with a name almost as long as the dog. Although Chihuahuas are usually shy and reserved and more at home in fast-food commercials, this event gives the little critters a chance to run rampantly through the streets.

Every year during the city's Cinco de Mayo celebration, the Chihuahuas compete for prizes, glory, and honor by entering king and queen contests and the grueling 10.7-meter dashes. The rewards include bejeweled sombreros, capes, and a chance to lord over the rest of their breed for the following year.

The race qualifiers run heats to determine the finalists. The track is a stretch of asphalt covered with sod and divided into five 35-foot lanes. Owners and trainers are allowed to urge their noble steeds on by waving toys, petit filet mignons, or rawhide bones at the finish line. Unfortunately Chihuahuas sometimes put appetite over loyalty, so it's not uncommon for an entrant to cut across the lanes to get to a turkey leg ahead of the rightful owner.

The field is gradually narrowed to five, and then the champion Chihuahua outruns the rest in the final heat of the day. The winner gets a 4-foot trophy; the winner's owner gets a medal and bragging rights.

For information on off-track Chihuahua betting, call (480) 963–3953.

S P O U T I N G   O F F   B I G T I M E
F o u n t a i n   H i l l s

What used to be the World's Tallest Fountain has been usurped by the Gateway Geyser in East St. Louis, Illinois, but the folks in Fountain Hills aren't surrendering the title without a fight. While they concede the geyser's 627-foot eruption may be taller, they are also quick to point out that the new titleholder spouts only from mid-April through mid-October. That factor makes it a part-time world's tallest, which means that for the other six months, the Fountain Hills spouter can lay claim to the honor.

When operating at full capacity, the World's Sometimes Tallest Fountain can blast a gusher of recycled water 560 feet into the air. That's higher than such other famous fountains as Le Jet d'Eau in Geneva, Switzerland (a 400-footer) and the Cap-

Fountain Hills used to have the world's tallest fountain, but now it has to settle for second place.

tain Cook Memorial Jet in Canberra, Australia (450 feet). Three 600-horsepower pumps shoot the 6-inch column of water through a nozzle that weighs more than a ton and measures 7 feet long.

However, there's another however. The Fountain Hills fountain operates at full strength only on such special occasions as the Fourth of July and St. Patrick's Day (when the spurt is colored green, naturally). The rest of the time it uses only two pumps, so the geyser averages about 330 feet.

Then, of course, there's always the question: How do they know how high it is? Nobody has ever shinnied up the column with a 560-foot tape measure. Parks and Recreation workers in charge of such perplexments say survey crews handle the task.

The fountain shot its first geyser skyward on December 15, 1970. It was installed by the McCulloch Corporation, the same folks who brought the London Bridge to Arizona. Initially it ran fifty-five minutes every hour, but now the eruptions occur every hour on the hour for fifteen to thirty minutes from 9:00 A.M. to 9:00 P.M. daily.

It's located on Saguaro Boulevard about 2 miles north of Shea Boulevard. You can't miss it. Just look to the squirted skies.

THE DINOSAUR'S JOURNEY
Fountain Hills

Despite the impression given in the *Jurassic Park* movies, dinosaurs don't always have things their own way. For example, there's one sitting in a park in Holbrook that was originally meant to be an outdoor shower near a Fountain Hills golf course. It lost the job because of a weight problem.

The odyssey started in 1997 when Jack and Joanne Lundeen and their daughter, Jeni, were browsing through an art gallery in New York, looking for art to install in the home they were building in Fountain Hills. After spotting a large bronze dinosaur sculpture, Jeni facetiously reminded her dad that she had a birthday coming up and a dinosaur is something every teenage girl really wants.

Jack Lundeen liked the idea of owning a dinosaur so they bought it, not as a gift for Jeni but for use as a shower next to their swimming pool. "Just think of it, water shooting out of a dinosaur's mouth," he said. The sculpture was shipped to Fountain Hills but had to be stored until the house was completed. When the time came to install the dinosaur-as-fountain, the Lundeens hired a crane to hoist it from the driveway over the house to the pool. But the crane boom was too short. And since that was the only way of relocating the dinosaur (it stands 9 feet tall and weighs about five tons), they opted to abandon the idea.

"We had stopped in Holbrook a couple of times," Lundeen said, "and noticed all the dinosaurs they have there, so we

When they couldn't find a crane big enough to install a five-ton bronze dinosaur as their outdoor shower, the Lundeen family of Fountain Hills donated it to the city of Holbrook as the centerpiece for a park.

decided to offer it to the city as a gift." The city readily accepted and sent a large truck and a crew of twenty men to retrieve it from the Lundeens' driveway and haul it back.

Now the much-traveled bronze beast sits in Living West Park on the corner of Hopi Street and Navajo Boulevard. And the only time it gets wet is when it rains in Holbrook.

OLD MCDONALD'S HAD A PIANO
Gilbert

The aroma is the same, the arches are the familiar golden yellow, and the burger servers look like thousands of others who dispense fast food all across the world. But still, there's something different about the McDonald's on Warner Road.

It's probably the piano.

Where other eateries of this genre devote space to playrooms and images of the frowzy-haired Ronald, this one offers music, played on a large piano that occupies a small stage in the center of the dining area. It's a modern-day version of the old player piano with a couple of notable exceptions. The old-timers were usually uprights; this one's a Grand. And the music comes from a compact disc player, not a roll with holes punched in it.

After buying the franchise, owner Michelle Adair and her parents, Ernie and Mary Adair, set out to drastically alter the standard McDonald's decor. They paid $25,000 for the piano and found other musical instruments and artworks to carry out the theme. So there's a saxophone hanging over the soft-drink machine, a cello over the cash register, and stylized treble clefs near the drive-in window. The walls are decorated with prints of young musicians and great musicians, and the booths are adorned with large quarter notes and sixteenth notes.

The piano plays CD-generated music most of the time, but occasionally manager Michael Brewer lets someone with known musical talent perform, provided they haven't been eating fries with ketchup.

The McDonald's is located on the northwest corner of Warner Road and Val Vista Drive in Gilbert. There's no admission fee for the concerts.

NOT YOUR RUN-OF-THE-MILL MILL
Gilbert

To Don and Carolyn Riedlinger, it's a dream come true. To several new brides, it's a place they'll always remember. To the average person who happens to drive by, it looks like something out of a picture book. Actually, it really is all those things, but in the shape of a gristmill.

Although it sits in what used to be Arizona desert, it's a real gristmill. Or, to be precise, it used to be a gristmill. It was built in Muddy Creek, Virginia, around 1842 and used old stone grinders to produce flour. A roller mill was installed in the 1920s to make finer, whiter flour. The building was rapidly decaying when the Riedlingers bought it in 1997.

"We took it apart and numbered and lettered every board," Don Riedlinger said. "Our blueprints for putting it back together were a throwaway camera and a spiral notebook." (Earlier the couple used that same technique to transfer a large barn to Gilbert from Iowa. It's now their home.) After two years the huge jigsaw puzzle was completed, and the gristmill was back in business, this time as a wedding place.

It's called the Shenandoah Mill now, and the wedding parties walk across hand-hewn wood floors and have their photos taken in front of the original waterwheel. An ancient engine and several grinding wheels give the grounds an old-fashioned air, while a stereo sound system, disc jockeys, and a vine-covered walkway and landscaped gardens bring it into this century.

The mill is at 1359 South Gilbert Road in Gilbert. For more information log on to www.shenandoahmill.com or call (480) 855–0099. And it's not necessary to say "I do" when they answer the phone.

Bugly but Not Ugly
Glendale

Nedra Solomon's grandchildren have it easy when it comes to gifts for Grandma. They catch bugs.

Solomon is the owner, curator, and tour guide at the Katydid Insect Museum, where the motto is "Come on in, let's take a tour; some of the insects have lots of allure." The establishment is a natural offshoot of her chosen profession. She and her husband have owned a pest-control business since 1968. "When other girls were choosing to be nurses and stenographers, I decided to become an exterminator," she said.

The museum has been open since 1999. It's already outgrown its quarters once, and a second expansion is in the works. It now contains more than 7,000 species of insect, most of which were captured by Nedra Solomon during working hours. But her collection also includes some exotic bugs from far away places, a few lizards, and a 6-foot iguana that she walks through the neighborhood on a leash. She buys about 1,000 crickets a week to keep her menagerie fed. Ironically, Solomon's not afraid of anything that crawls over and under the earth, but she has a major fear of birds.

Not all her displays are garden-variety bugs, however. One is a 6-inch walking stick in a plastic case. Four of her grand-

Nedra Solomon doesn't fear bugs, but birds aren't welcome in Katydid Insect Museum in Glendale.

daughters chipped in and paid $200 for it. "But the little ones, they just tell each other to find me some bugs for Christmas and birthday gifts," she said.

The place is extremely popular with children who aren't old enough to realize that bugs are ugly. Squishy, perhaps, but not ugly.

The museum, at 5060 West Bethany Home Road in Glendale, is open Monday through Friday from 11:00 A.M. to 4:30 P.M. For details, call (623) 931–8718 or log on to www.insect museum.com. Admission fees vary.

LOOK! UP IN THE SKY! IT'S A
FLYING FARMALL!
Glendale

Larry Rovey says the reason for the tractor on the flagpole is simple: He always wanted to see what it'd look like if he put one up there.

The tractor is a 1920s Farmall Regular, and it's mounted on the flagpole in front of Rovey Dairy. It sits about 20 feet off the ground on a steel post that used to be a utility pole. The area underneath the tractor-on-a-stick is filled with other pieces of old equipment, all part of Rovey's collection. He owns more than 200 vintage tractors, plows, discs, hay rakes, seeders, and other implements that once tilled the soil. His long-range plan is to build an agricultural heritage museum and stock it with his antiques.

Rovey said getting the Farmall onto the flagpole was "terribly simple," but it took some ingenuity and heavy equipment. After digging a big hole, a crew managed to stand the post upright and secure it, but they still faced the problem of hoisting the tractor to its new location near the top. Fortunately there was a utility crew working in the area, so Rovey asked them for help. They volunteered a crane and several operators and raised the old tractor to new heights without a hitch.

Anyone interested in seeing a tractorsicle will find this one at 7711 West Northern on the western edge of Glendale.

To Bead or Not to Bead Is Not the Question
Glendale

The Bead Museum traces its history to the slave traders and a buying mistake. Back in 1969, Gabrielle Liese ordered what she thought was a shade pull from a catalog. But when it arrived, she discovered it was actually a bead necklace. Intrigued, she researched the beads and found out they were millefiori Venetians, once used as currency by ancient Venetian traders when buying gold, salt, and slaves.

Intrigued by all this, Liese began acquiring beads from across the world. When her collection exceeded the living space in her home, she opened a small shop in Prescott. That also became too small, so she moved the facility to Glendale in 1999.

Now she's the curator of one of the world's few museums devoted to the history of the bead. She has collected 8,000-year-old obsidian beads and 10,000-year-old bone and shell beads. Other exhibits illustrate authentic beads vs. imitations, an overview of the use of beads in various cultures, and an estimated 100,000 beads from throughout the world.

The museum also offers beading classes and a gift shop. It's located at 5754 West Glenn Drive in Glendale. The phone number is (623) 931-2737. They're always glad to help, even if you ask, "Will you bead my Valentine?"

A SPOT TO HISS IN
Goldfield Ghost Town

Creepy crawly things need friends, too. Zach Ziesing lets them crawl down his arms and across his hands, and he doesn't even flinch or worry about warts.

Ziesing is the proprietor of the Superstition Reptile Exhibit at the Goldfield Ghost Town, a tourist attraction. He is therefore the caretaker of ninety different species of creatures that crawl and slither and slime and repel, everything from Gila monsters to tarantulas to rattlesnakes.

"I focus on venomous animals of the Sonoran Desert," he said while retrieving a 9-inch multilegged wormlike thing from its glass cage so he could give a bunch of high-school girls a reason to overdose on high-pitched screams.

Ziesing handles many of his charges like pets but warns his visitors not to try it at home, because he is a professional and they probably aren't. His exhibit is open daily, but there's no phone at the exhibit because snakes, as a rule, don't want to be bothered by picking one up and saying, "Who hiss this?"

The ghost town is at 4650 North Mammoth Mine Road on Highway 88 northeast of Apache Junction. For details, call (480) 983–0333.

ON BEING A BIG BABY
Goodyear

Sometimes, art shows up in the strangest places. An example is the big baby in the middle of a plowed field in a semirural area north of Interstate 10. Even though seated, the child—a girl—is about 12 feet tall, and she's playing with some adult dolls.

Huge plywood cutouts attract freeway gawkers
along Interstate 10 in Goodyear.

They're all plywood cutouts, skillfully painted on the side facing the freeway, but just plain wood on the other side. They, and several other pieces a couple of miles up the road, are the work of California artist John Cerney, who used photographs of real people as models. The land is on Duncan Family Farms property, and the little girl depicted is Jaymee Lawton. She's the granddaughter of Bob and Gratia Sheppard, longtime friends of Kathleen Duncan, one of the owners. Duncan and Bob Sheppard are both depicted as dolls in the setting.

The works were put up in the field around 1997 and require constant upkeep due to weather and vandalism. "They don't have any real meaning," said Gratia Sheppard. "It's just fun art."

The cutouts are located on the north side of I–10 near the Cotton Lane exit, so they're visible only from the westbound lane. And always remember to look fast. Regular freeway users don't exhibit much patience with art lovers.

FOR THE LOVE OF THE GAME
Phoenix

Like most people, Todd McFarlane collects things. In his case, it's baseballs.

Expensive baseballs.

McFarlane deals in quality, not quantity. He owns only ten baseballs, but his collection is worth an estimated $4 million. Most of it (more than $3 million) went for the purchase of the ball Mark McGwire hit over the fence for his seventieth home run in 1998. The St. Louis Cardinals slugger had earlier surpassed the single season four-bagger record of 61, set by Roger Maris of the New York Yankees in 1961. McFarlane also owns six other McGwire home-run balls from that same year, as well as three that were belted into the stands by Sammy Sosa of the Chicago Cubs as the two battled for all-time homer-king honors. McGwire's record lasted less than three years. Barry Bonds of the San Francisco Giants hit seventy-three in 2002.

McFarlane can afford his passion. He is the creator of the *Spawn* comic book series, which has spawned a big-screen movie plus figurines of his comic-book characters, sports figures, and rock musicians that are sold all over the world.

He has no plans to sell off his collection, saying he'd rather keep all ten together and work out an arrangement with the Baseball Hall of Fame, in Cooperstown, New York, to put them on permanent display.

RECYCLED SKELETONS
Phoenix

Bruce Law's front yard looks like the place where old saguaro cacti go to die. Skeletons of the once-noble plants, stacked as neatly as they can be considering their shape, occupy a major portion of his north Phoenix property.

Law uses his skill as a wood-carver to resurrect them into pieces of fine art. He doesn't use the entire skeleton, just the area where an arm once sprouted from the trunk. There's a large piece of wood at each intersection, and it yields easily to Law's knives. He carves a human face or the head of a bird or animal, and then lets the flow of the ribs become hair, mane, or feathers.

He starts by cutting a skeleton arm in half. Is he looking for an image trapped in the wood? "Naaah, hell no," he said. "I'm just trying to figure out if there's enough wood to carve a face."

It's illegal to remove saguaro skeletons from public lands, but Law has an ample supply on property owned by friends. He also works to preserve the huge saguaros. He plants arms from fire-damaged saguaros and acts as a nursemaid until they take root. Many of them have survived.

Once he finishes a saguaro carving, Law airbrushes the highlights, turns it over to a gallery, and hopes it sells for his asking price, which goes as high as $1,500.

HOW IT ALL BEGAN
Phoenix

Like most boys, George Getz wanted a fire truck for Christmas. Unlike most boys, he got one. A couple of other twists make the story notable. One is that Getz was an adult boy of forty-five years at the time. The other is that the fire engine he received was a real one, a 1924 LaFrance American, and it was a gift from his wife, not his parents.

The family was living in Lake Geneva, Illinois, in 1951 when Getz expressed the desire to own a fire engine. His wife, Olive, found one and hired a fireman to drive it 300 miles to their home, where she wrapped a pretty good size bow around it and hid it in a service station until Christmas morning.

The result of that less-than-humble beginning is the Hall of Flame, the world's largest firefighting museum. After receiving the LaFrance truck, Getz began collecting in earnest. He opened the museum in Illinois, then moved it to Phoenix in 1974. It started as one building and about 10,000 square feet. Now it is 52,000 square feet and contains 104 firefighting rigs, from horse-drawn units to hand pumpers, as well as other equipment and a Hall of Heroes that honors firemen for heroic deeds.

When George Getz asked for a fire engine as a
Christmas present, this is what he got. The Hall of
Flame in Phoenix was the inevitable result.

George Getz died in 1992 at age eighty-three. His grandson,
also George Getz, now heads the operation.

The museum is at 6101 East Van Buren. For details, call
(602) 275–3473.

A CROWNING PLACE
Phoenix

The Castle on Camelback Mountain comes up for sale every now and then. The last asking price was $8 million. It's a fair amount, considering the castle features 8,000 square feet of living space, an indoor pool, a waterfall, and a spectacular view about 600 feet above the rest of the area.

Dr. Mort Koppenhaver built the place pretty much by himself back in the late 1960s and early 1970s. He was a dentist who worked at fixing teeth in the mornings and creating his dream house in the afternoons. He blasted rock from Camelback Mountain to make a road and then used the blasted rock as building material for the castle. The construction went on for eleven years.

Koppenhaver said he needed help only when it came time to hoist the massive beams that hold up the ceiling. When his castle was completed, he lived in it for a while and threw some royal parties. But, unlike the castle occupants who thrive in fairy tales, he didn't get to live there happily ever after. He put the property up as collateral for a business venture. It failed and he lost the castle. It has had several owners since.

The castle is on the south side of Camelback Mountain, north of Camelback Road between Forty-sixth Street and Launfal Street. It's a bit difficult to spot during the daytime; the rock walls blend into the color of the mountain because they were originally part of the mountain. But it's quite visible at night, because there are lights all over the place. You can drive close and take a look, but it's not open to the public.

TAKE ME OUT TO THE SWIMMING POOL
Phoenix

There's a new tradition at the old ballpark here—bobbing for baseballs. It probably won't catch on anywhere else, however. It requires a major-league baseball park equipped with a swimming pool, and there's only one of them in the country.

The pool is located beyond the fence in right center field at the Bank One Ballpark, where the Arizona Diamondbacks won the World Series in 2001. The area contains both a pool and a hot tub and can hold thirty-five scantily clad fans. Jerry Colangelo, Diamondbacks managing general partner and the man responsible for bringing major-league baseball to Arizona, said the idea sprang from a fans' shower installed in Chicago's Comiskey Park by Bill Veeck when he owned the Chicago White Sox. Veeck assumed that some fans might need to wash up after a game, particularly if they'd had frequent contact with the beer salesmen.

The pool rents for more than $5,500 a day (or night), and it has been a sellout for every game since the ballpark opened in 1998. Corporations are the primary users, but one fan rented it for his own birthday party.

Occasionally a player will disrupt the pool party by whacking a home run into the water. It has happened, but fewer than thirty-five times after five full seasons. It takes a pretty good poke to dunk one, because it's 405 feet from home plate to pool.

On rare occasions a watery homer means a new car for a lucky fan. If a player belts one into the pool during a designated inning of a designated game, a designated fan gets a new Nissan Xterra. That has also occurred, but only twice.

For more information on watching baseball in a bikini, call (602) 514–8400 and select option 5 or log on to www.azdiamondbacks.com.

NO JOB SECURITY HERE

*I*n most states, getting yourself elected governor means regular paychecks and good perks for the duration. Not in Arizona. In the past three decades, only two of those elevated to the state's highest position have served full terms.

This trend toward nonlongevity started in 1974 when Raul Castro was elected. He took office in 1975 but served only until October 22, 1977, when he resigned to become U.S. ambassador to Argentina. Wesley Bolin, the secretary of state, was appointed governor.

Bolin died on March 4, 1978, only five months into his term. Normally, the secretary of state would have replaced him. But because Rose Mofford had been appointed to replace Bolin, she could not ascend to the governor's chair since the order of succession requires that the person filling the governor's unexpired term must be elected. So Mofford was passed over in favor of Bruce Babbitt, the elected attorney general.

Babbitt served the rest of the Castro/Bolin term and won two more terms, serving through 1986. Evan Mecham was elected in 1986, took office in 1987, but lasted only until April 4, 1988, when he was ousted after being convicted in a Senate impeachment trial of obstructing justice and misusing public funds. Rose Mofford, now having been duly elected as secretary of state, was appointed governor. She completed the term but didn't run again.

Fife Symington was elected in 1990 and 1994, but a U.S. District Court jury convicted him on September 3, 1997 of defrauding lenders during his previous career as a developer. He resigned two days later, leaving the chair to Secretary of State Jane Hull. She finished that term but chose not to run again.

Janet Napolitano won the governorship in the November 2002 election, but the voting was so close she wasn't declared the winner until five days after the polls closed.

Stay tuned.

S o W H E R E ' S T H E S P H I N X ?
P h o e n i x

L ike Cairo, Egypt, Phoenix is a desert city. So it's only natural that they both have pyramids. Cairo wins the Biggest Pyramid Contest hands down, however. The Phoenix entry is merely a four-sided, pointy anthill by comparison. But it does have an interesting story behind its beginnings.

The pyramid is called Hunt's Tomb and most believe it's a monument to George West Hunt, who served seven two-year terms as Arizona's governor. He was first elected in 1912 and re-elected in 1914. In 1916 he lost to Thomas Campbell by thirty votes. But then Hunt wouldn't leave. He said Campbell had run illegally, so he locked him out of the office. Campbell started governing from his own home and, for a month, the state labored under two leaders. The courts finally came down on Campbell's side but Hunt sued. Eleven months later, the Arizona Supreme Court booted out Campbell and restored Hunt.

Campbell was eventually elected and served two terms before Hunt regained the throne and served until 1928.

But back to the pyramid that bears his name. Hunt built the monument as a tomb for his wife, Helen, who died in 1931. He got the idea while on a trip to Egypt and after his wife's burial, he noted that there was room for several more bodies inside. His mother-in-law had died in 1929, and both Hunt and his father-in-law passed away in 1934, so all three were interred in the tomb. His wife's sister was buried there in 1953, and the ashes of Virginia Hunt, his daughter, and her husband were placed inside in 1985.

The tomb is located in Papago Park and, somewhat fittingly, now overlooks the Phoenix Zoo.

LASER BOMBARDMENT

*A*ny mention of Arizona's gubernatorial shortcomings and unfulfillments should include the Laser Beam Incident.

Just before he was removed from his term as governor in 1988, Evan Mecham told associates that he couldn't talk openly in his office. He claimed that one of his eavesdropping political foes had laser beams pointed at his windows.

Fortunately for the sake of office secrecy, Mecham also claimed he could deflect the beams by varying the volume of his radio while he talked.

JACOB'S LAST WALTZ
Phoenix

*A*lthough he's been in his grave for more than a century, Jacob Waltz is still a pretty good source of revenue.

Waltz is the key figure in the legend of the Lost Dutchman Mine, a shadowy place where the gold allegedly jumps out of the ground and into the pockets of those who stumble across it. He was a German immigrant who prospected in the Superstition Mountains. According to the folklore, Waltz made regular trips into the mountains and always returned with large amounts of high-grade gold ore.

Some historians believe he found a rich mine abandoned by the Peralta family of Mexico. Others say it was gold hidden by the Apaches after they massacred a group of Mexican miners.

Nobody knows for sure because Waltz wasn't the kind of guy who'd toss out hints about his secret hiding places. He made vague references to the mine's location, but he never gave details to anyone.

After his death in 1891, Waltz and his gold mine became a cottage industry. Several books purport to describe the exact location of the mine. Several prospectors claim they've found the mine but need grubstake money to work it. And almost every souvenir shop in Phoenix hawks treasure maps that supposedly reveal precisely which shadow of which peak points to the mine at a certain time of day.

So while the writers and mapmakers prosper, Jacob Waltz's remains lie in an almost-neglected grave in the Pioneer and Military Memorial Park in Phoenix. Even today there's an air of secrecy about the man and the legend. The park is near the State Capitol, but it takes an appointment to get past the four locked gates that guard the gravesite. Those interested can call (602) 534-1262.

LOUIS LEE'S LABOR OF LOVE
Phoenix

Louis Lee spent more than forty years creating his masterpiece. It may or may not be art, depending upon the audience. But it sure is interesting.

In 1958 Lee bought a house in what was then a sparsely populated area of north Phoenix. After moving his family in, he scoured the nearby hills for small rocks and used them to build things in his yard—arches, walls, shrines, small temples, grottoes, and walkways.

Lee purchased small statues of Buddha, elephants, lions, and

*Phoenician Louis Lee has spent most of his life working
on his rock garden, combining stones and cactus with
newspaper clippings and statues in a work of art.*

dragons and incorporated them into his stonework. Then he
started adding other items, like newspaper clippings, photographs, vases, hubcaps, a toilet seat, tin signs, and tiles. Next he
planted trees, cacti, and shrubs and installed a watering system.

"I had no plan," Lee said. "I just kept building." Eventually
the project took up all his available space. Now his entire front
yard, from his house to the street, is covered with his stone art.
Lee, a retired artist who turned eighty-nine in 2002, calls it
The Lee Oriental Rock Garden.

Most of his material came from the neighborhood, but one
area displays rocks his son brought home from the Great Wall

of China. "I went there a couple of times," Lee said, "but I didn't get any rocks. I didn't want to explain to customs that I was bringing home rocks from China."

The garden is at 4015 East McDonald Drive. It's not open to the public, but those who approach the house and ask nicely often get a guided tour led by the artist himself. Groups should write first to ask for an appointment. The zip code is 85018.

SQUEEZIN' FOR PEACE
Phoenix

Bill Molnar doesn't think warfare is a good way to attain world peace. He believes the accordion works just as well. And on a small scale, he's trying to prove his point.

He started playing the squeezebox more than seventy years ago as part of a boys band in Cleveland, Ohio. Now it's his traveling companion. "When I'm in a different country, I never know the language so I play the accordion," he said. "Everybody understands the accordion."

He has staged impromptu concerts throughout Europe and Asia. "I did 'O Sole Mio' at a sidewalk cafe in Rome and 'Under Paris Skies' at one in Paris," he said. "I played 'My Wild Irish Rose' at Tiananmen Square in Beijing, and the people always smile. They mistake me for Lawrence Welk."

He has also played while waiting in line at McDonald's in Moscow, on the major thoroughfares of Shanghai, in front of the opera house in Sydney, Australia, for monks in Tibet, and for children in Ethiopia. When he can't take his own accordion along, he finds a music store and rents one. And, he adds, the response is always positive.

In 1988 he borrowed a raccoon coat and porkpie hat and accompanied former Arizona governor Bruce Babbitt on a presidential campaign tour through New Hampshire. His playing received almost as much news coverage as the candidate.

Then he decided to become an actor, so he hired an agent, had some publicity stills taken, and broke into films, appearing as a janitor in *Waiting to Exhale* and a barfly in *The Gambler*. Later he joined the entertainment staff of a cruise ship for a summer.

After that he read about Mother Theresa's charity work, so he flew by himself to Calcutta, found her mission, and spent nearly a month as one of her volunteers. Now he's a regular guest artist at nursing homes around Phoenix.

"I try to stay active," he said. "When I go to a different country, I may not speak the language but my accordion transcends all barriers. And I've never had a tomato thrown at me."

CASTLE OR GIANT WEDDING CAKE?
Phoenix

The Tovrea Castle has been a Phoenix landmark ever since Alessio Carraro decided to build a structure that resembled a huge wedding cake. Carraro, an Italian immigrant, left a successful business in San Francisco and started the project in 1928. He bought 277 acres of desert and set about creating a hotel that would serve as an anchor for a planned housing subdivision. He figured his guests would become so enamored with the surroundings that they'd readily buy a lot so they could stay forever.

Working without plans or construction drawings, Carraro created the structure in the form of four elongated octagons sitting on top of each another. He surrounded the building with elaborate cactus gardens, boulders, pathways, and fishponds and called it Carraro Heights.

But it was not to be. Immediately west of the castle was a forty-acre buffer zone that separated Carraro's dream from E. A. Tovrea's packing plant and feeder lots. Carraro had tried to buy the property, but it was sold to Tovrea, who promptly began installing sheep pens. Since very few hotel guests enjoyed sharing the desert air with sheep pens, the maneuver spelled the end of Carraro's development.

Then in 1931 Carraro unwittingly sold his castle and gardens to Tovrea's spouse, Della, and the couple moved right in. Tovrea died in 1932; his widow lived there until her death in 1969.

The city of Phoenix purchased the castle and part of the grounds in 1993 and has been buying more of the property ever since. The eventual goal is permanent use as a diplomatic reception center. There are no plans, however, to change the name to Carraro Castle.

Fans of wedding-cake architecture can view the four-tiered dream house on Van Buren Street between Forty-eighth and Fifty-second Streets in east Phoenix.

STUFF YOUR OWN
Phoenix

The allure of owning a teddy bear is universal, but stuffing your very own bear makes it even specialer, a word not found in the dictionary but common among bear stuffers who visit the Stuffington Bear Factory.

For a fee, bear fanciers of all ages can select an empty bear hide and guide it through the six-step process to bring it to life, so to speak. Although it's mostly automated, the new bear owner gets to watch and supervise as the bear is stuffed, brushed, vacuumed, dressed, and given a name. The procedure takes about twenty minutes. Each bear comes with a birth certificate and two ribbons. Some buy bear clothing, others prefer to leave their bears bare. Except for the ribbons.

The factory is open daily for both drop-in and scheduled tours. Tours last about twenty-five minutes and give the guests a firsthand look at how other bears get stuffed and how they put the eyes in. Most of the tourists are children, but retirees also make frequent visits. Those planning a trip should call first because, after twenty-four years in the same location at 2645 East Washington, the factory may be forced to move. If that happens, find out where the new one is located by calling (602) 225–9513, or log on to www.stuffington.com.

ALICE STILL LIVES HERE ANYMORE
Phoenix

The dress code at Alice Cooper'stown is somewhere between ultracasual and superrelaxed for both clientele and staff, so the only thing that sets the place apart from most others of its kind is the eye makeup. All the servers apply it so they sort of resemble Alice Cooper, the rock legend who is also a principal owner of the night club/restaurant/sports bar.

Cooper, known for his outlandish cosmetics during his long run as a pop star, was there on opening night in November 1998, and all the servers put on eye shadow to honor the boss. Customers liked the idea so much that it became a standard, and now servers roam the premises wearing black Cooper marks around their eyes.

The establishment's decor combines rock 'n' roll and sports memorabilia with twenty-four big-screen television sets. One that stretches across the entire back bar can serve as sixteen big screens, four extrabig screens, or one humongous screen that is said to be the largest in the western United States and most of northern Mexico.

If you visit, you might mention that you know his real name isn't Alice Cooper. He's actually Vincent Damon Furnier, a Detroit native who grew up in Phoenix and formed a band called the Spiders in 1965. It won't get you a free beer, but it might impress some of your friends.

Alice Cooper'stown is located on the southeast corner of Jackson and First Street downtown.

Alice Cooper's outlandish makeup is partially emulated by loyal employees at AliceCooper'stown, a nightclub in downtown Phoenix.

WHEN THE CITY WENT TO POT(S)
Phoenix

The official project name is "Wall Cycle to Ocotillo," but very few call it that. To most, it's the "Freeway Pots," a title administered during an "art is in the eye of the beholder" ruckus shortly after the artwork was installed.

Back in 1992 the city of Phoenix laid out $474,000 for an arts project designed to enhance the Squaw Peak Parkway. It was the city's first attempt at highway beautification, but it almost backfired because it consisted of thirty-five pots. Big pots, little pots, pots that look like teapots, and pots that look like giant flower vases. The public ridiculed the design, the price tag, and the selection of out-of-state artists to create the pieces. At one point an anonymous dissenter placed a toilet that had been spray painted gold on top of a wall to mock one pot that, according to some, resembled a commode.

The backlash forced the Phoenix City Council to change its policy on public art, adding emphasis to in-state artists and giving the community and council members more input on art selection. But the pots are still there, and they've received favorable attention from the national media.

The vessels are polychrome concrete and painted steel, and range in size from 2 feet to 15 feet. Only six are visible from the freeway; the rest are on side streets and bike paths on both sides of the thoroughfare. They start just south of McDowell Road and run north to Ocotillo Road. Some of the pots were removed and put in storage due to a freeway widening project in 2003. Their fate is uncertain.

For more information on this or any of the other seventy-five public arts projects in Phoenix, call (602) 262–4637.

THE FAKE FIREHOUSE
Phoenix

There's this firehouse on Roeser Road that looks exactly like a firehouse, but it isn't. It's a trick. It's really a building painted to look like an old firehouse, and the artist did such an excellent job that, from a distance, it looks exactly like a firehouse, complete with old fire engines standing ready to honk and blare and a Dalmatian dog waiting by the doorway.

The illusion, called trompe l'oeil (French for "fools the eye"), was applied to the 2-story building by artist Richard Haas in 1985, when the Thunderbird Fire and Safety Equipment Corporation occupied the structure. When that firm left in 2001, the building was sold to Clear Connection, LLC. The new owners elected to leave the paint job intact because of its public appeal.

And the fact that some of Haas' other work is getting national attention.

Haas' paint job gives the impression that the viewer is looking at a sandstone-block building. To enhance the effect, he painted rocks at the base that blend into the real rocks used in the landscaping, put in arched doors and windows, and worked his artistry all the way around the corner, where the illusion ends. The final section was left unfinished. It shows two painted painters on painted scaffolding. And they are painting a building to look like an old firehouse.

The nonarsonous work of art is at 3440 East Roeser Road. You won't have to stop for the fire engines, but you should stop for a closer look.

THE SANDY RIVER ESCAPADE

*T*he largest prisoner-of-war escape ever staged inside the United States failed because rivers aren't always blue.

In December 1944, twenty-five German POWs escaped from the military prison in Papago Park. Most of them had served on U-boats and had been sent to the Arizona desert to get them as far away from water as possible. The escapees had dug a 180-foot tunnel under the prison to the Arizona Crosscut Canal, one of several irrigation ditches that run through the Phoenix area.

Prior to the flight three prisoners built a small boat that they smuggled out with them. Using maps they had pilfered while on work details outside the prison camp, they planned an escape route down the canals to the Salt and Gila Rivers and then on to Yuma, from where they'd take the Colorado River into Mexico. But the flaw in their plan was that although they appear as blue lines on maps, Arizona's rivers rarely have water in them. So when the trio got to the river, it was a dry bed and none of them ever got to Mexico.

Within days all but one of the escapees was recaptured. The first returnee, in fact, came back voluntarily. He told authorities he preferred the camp's Christmas dinner to what he was likely to get on the outside. Captain Jurgen Wattenburg, their leader, hid out until the following spring; he was captured when he asked a gas station attendant for directions to the train station.

A WHALE OF A QUAIL
Phoenix

Hunters often stop at Kelly Woodson's place and ask if they can have their pictures taken with his quail. It seems to give them a sense of accomplishment because the quail is 8 feet tall, and hunters like to put "bagged an 8-foot quail" on their resumes.

It's not uncommon for hunters to stop at Kelly Woodson's house in Phoenix and ask to have their pictures taken with his giant quail.

The big bird was manufactured by a Phoenix float-building company and was originally part of a float that appeared in a Rose Bowl Parade. Larry Woodson, Kelly's father, acquired two of them in the late 1980s when the float builders went out of business. He gave one away as a wedding gift and planted the other one in his front yard. It's been there ever since, except for the time it was kidnapped. "I called the police and gave them a description of an 8-foot quail," he said and chuckled. "They didn't sound like they believed me but four hours later they found it in an alley. They loaded it up and brought it back."

When the elder Woodson moved away, his son inherited both the house and its oversized watchbird. They're both standing near the corner of Carson Street and Fair Lane, just off Forty-eighth Street in Phoenix.

ONE MAN'S TREASURES
Phoenix

"I t'll take me another twenty years to get it the way I want it," Gus Brethauer said during a tour through the vast collection of acrylic grapes, tiled walls, petrified wood, boulders, UFOs, wrought-iron fencing, and other items he calls "Somewhere Over the Rainbow, a study in stone, in color and theme without equal or parallel on the face of the earth."

He's been working on this project, which he claims is the world's largest privately owned amusement park, for about fifty years. If he finishes on schedule, he'll be age ninety-eight when it's done. Then what? "Oh, I'll probably expand," he said. "There's a lot of stuff I don't have on display yet."

What he currently has on display is an eclectic assortment of multi-ton rocks, archways made of oil drums, plaster birds and plastic bunnies, more than 1,000 plants, building blocks, tree stumps, and dinosaurs both large and small. "I spent

He's not exactly Indiana Jones, but Gus Brethauer seeks out antiquities
in some unlikely places. Here he stands with his pet triceratops.

almost a million dollars creating this place," Brethauer said
with unconcealed pride, "and this is what I got to show for it."

His park is in a residential area surrounded by 2-story
houses that look down on his collection, including the swamp
he fills only when important visitors request an audience. He
can't charge admission but if a guest wants to slip him a $20,
he's not above accepting it as a donation.

The tour can last anywhere between an hour and three
hours, depending on how Gus feels that day. There's a story
behind every cactus, every drill bit, the haunted house, and the
piece of pie in that old refrigerator, and Brethauer is eager to
tell them. Every one of them.

Those interested in spending half a day in a three-acre naive fantasyland can call Gus at (602) 992–1669. If he doesn't answer, keep trying. It's worth the effort.

THE FIGHTING ARTICHOKES
Salt River–Pima Maricopa Indian Community

The Scottsdale Community College athletic teams are nick-named the Artichokes. It's a classic case of turning a lemon into lemonade. Or in this case, an artichoke into art.

This journey into the world of jockstrap-wearing vegetables began during the school's formative years in the early 1970s. A dispute arose between students and the administration about which should be more important—athletics or academics. The administration wanted to emphasize athletics to attract media attention and income. The students envisioned more money for classrooms, scholarships, and learning.

The constitution gave students a voice in budget matters, but when the school built a $1.7 million gymnasium without their approval, the Artichoke Movement formed. In an apparent peacemaking attempt, the administration asked the student government to hold an election to select a mascot. Infuriated, the senate reacted by giving the students three choices—the Artichoke, the Rutabaga, or the Scoundrel. The Artichoke won, but the administration declared the election invalid.

After months of bickering, another election approved the Artichoke and also picked pink and green as the school colors. The administration balked at pink as a school color, however, so the teams became the blue-and-white-clad Artichokes, hardly a fashion statement.

Ironically the episode produced what school officials were looking for—publicity. The name has attracted international

Scottsdale Community College student Michel Leckband is an exemplification of the school's mascot, the Fighting Artichoke.

attention and is a frequent subject for both electronic and print media. And in 2002 the institution introduced a line of Artie Artichoke dolls as a marketing gimmick.

The school also had a mascot who showed up at football games wearing a homemade artichoke costume. School lore says he was dismissed because he never washed his uniform and, as most gourmets know, there's nothing worse than an overripe artichoke. The wife of a faculty member created a new costume that is still in use.

Vegetarian jocks can find more information at www.sc. maricopa.edu. The school is located at 9000 East Chaparral Road in the Salt River–Pima Maricopa Community along the 101 Freeway.

THE ONGOING NECKTIE PARTY
Scottsdale

Back in the good old days, when neckties were a popular gift item because they cost only a buck, going to the Pinnacle Peak Patio was a popular way to get rid of the ugly ones.

It was a simple procedure: Go there, order a steak, and get your necktie lopped off. This has been going on since 1957, when the original owners implemented a no-necktie policy. It was a small store then, selling food, beer, and bait to fishermen. But its beef dinners became so popular that it evolved into a steakhouse that cut off neckties.

According to lore, the first victims were a group of Phoenix businessmen who wandered into the place to eat lunch. When they lost their ties to the scissors, they demanded recognition for their sacrifice, so their neckwear was stapled to the rafters. The practice has continued for almost fifty years.

Now there are more than a million tie remnants hanging from the rafters. And there are lots of rafters. The patio calls itself the world's largest steakhouse containing the world's largest collection of no-longer-usable neckties. The million-necktie figure may not be accurate, but nobody disputes it. The diners are so involved in chomping down on their rares and medium rares they don't want to stop to count to one million. Since the staff claims that the place has served more than eleven million pounds of beef since 1957, they're way too busy to make the effort. So just accept it—there's a million ties hanging up there. And most of them are ugly.

Actor Patrick Swayze, singer Tanya Tucker, and motorist Mario Andretti are among the more notable of the tie-lopped. They probably paid more than $1.00 for their neckties, however.

Pinnacle Peak Patio is located at 10426 East Jomax Road in north Scottsdale. To make reservations for an ascotectomy procedure, call (480) 585–1599.

TRAVELING WITH LIZARDS
Scottsdale

By its own admission, Scottsdale does not tolerate mediocrity. This partially explains why there are giant lizards climbing the walls along a 6-mile stretch of the Pima Freeway as it courses its way along the city's eastern boundary.

When the Arizona Department of Transportation eliminated aesthetic-enhancement funds prior to construction of the freeway, the city elected to pay for its own artwork. It allocated $2.15 million for the project and selected Carolyn Braaksma of Denver for her design concept of a desert theme that included cacti, flora and fauna, lizards, and abstract Native American motifs.

STATELY BUT DEADLY

One thing newcomers to Arizona should learn in a hurry if they don't want to be mistaken for a newcomer is how to pronounce "saguaro," that towering cactus that is the state's unofficial symbol. It's "sa-WAR-o." In some areas of the state, "sa-HWAR-o" is acceptable. But no place in Arizona accepts "sag-U-arrow," "sag-U-ware-o" or any derivative thereof.

Even though they can stand as tall as 70 feet and weigh up to 10 tons, saguaros are continually under attack by humans. Until 1992, destroying or mutilating saguaros on state or public land was merely a misdemeanor. Now, however, the crime is a felony and those convicted draw fines of up to $100,000 plus three years in jail.

It's also illegal to destroy a saguaro even if you own it. Property owners can be fined up to $500 for improperly disposing of one on their land. They must first request a notice of intent, a process that gives the state time to post a notice for interested parties and salvage operators who might be interested in saving the cactus.

Another thing about this Arizona icon: Because a mature saguaro can weigh up to ten tons, it's not wise to go around picking on them—they've been known to fight back.

In 1982 a man used a shotgun to mutilate one of the giants in the Sonoran Desert near Phoenix. By peppering its base with slugs from a 16-gauge shotgun, he weakened the 26-foot cactus so much that it toppled over and crushed its antagonist.

Later that same year a glider pilot had to make an emergency landing, also in the Sonoran Desert north of Phoenix. The glider crashed into a saguaro and the impact caused the cactus to fall over on top of the aircraft, killing the pilot.

Work on the stretch of freeway began in 1966 and was completed in 2002. The artwork is on both sides of the noise abatement and retention walls, some of which rise 50 feet above the freeway. With that much space to work with, the designers were able to craft what may be the world's largest lizard, a 67-footer clinging to a concrete barrier.

The reason behind putting lizards and cacti on the walls is perhaps best summed up in this line from the design statement: "The monotony of mundane surroundings need not belong on (the) journey. Regardless of length, each journey should be a positive experience, with the constant possibilities of adventure and discovery."

THE SPLINTER ON ICE
Scottsdale

When baseball legend Ted Williams died on July 5, 2002, a logical choice for his final resting place would have seemed to be somewhere in Massachusetts, where he starred for the Boston Red Sox. Or California, where he grew up. Or even Florida, where he spent his final years.

But his remains are in Arizona. Frozen in the desert.

His body is floating upside down in a liquid nitrogen tank at Alcor Life Extension Foundation in Scottsdale. Two of his children had it placed there because they said they wanted the body preserved and later thawed or possibly cloned. Another child fought the decision, saying that in his will, Williams wanted cremation instead of refrigeration. The siblings took their battle to the courts, and the eventual ruling was that the slugger had changed his mind prior to heart surgery.

The freezing process, known as cryogenics or cryonic suspension, has long been a subject for debate. Proponents say a frozen body could possibly be restored if a cure is ever found for whatever caused the death. Dissenters say it's an impossible dream. According to news reports, Alcor has more than 50 bodies already frozen and another 580 living clients awaiting the process after their deaths. The cost, as of 2002, was $120,000 for the entire body or $50,000 for just the head. Nobody knows yet if it works.

Williams, dubbed "the Splendid Splinter" by sportswriters, was elected to the Baseball Hall of Fame and was the last major leaguer to bat over .400 for an entire season. During his lifetime he often described himself as an atheist who believed "when you're gone, you're gone."

HOME FOR A PRINCESS
South Mountain Regional Park

Boyce Luther Gulley was a recycler long before recycling became the in thing. He never threw anything away and, equally important, he put his treasures back into service by building a castle.

In one respect Gulley wasn't an ideal father. He disappeared in 1930, leaving a wife and daughter behind in Seattle, and the family didn't know where he'd gone until after his death in 1945. But he spent most of those fifteen years building a castle for his little girl. They used to make sand castles on the Washington beaches; she'd cry when the water washed them away, so he promised to build one that would last. It sits on a mountainside near South Mountain Regional Park and is a steady source of income for his daughter, Mary Lou Gulley, who leads tours through the house known as Mystery Castle.

Visitors get to see elder Gulley's assortment of Indian baskets and rugs, the Cactus Room, the Stairway to the Rainbow, the wedding chapel, and the Dug Out, a sunken bar. His building materials included an old car, stone, and rescued bricks. The structure contains eighteen rooms, thirteen fireplaces, nooks, crannies, and parapets.

The monument to a little girl is located at 800 East Mineral. Take Seventh Street south to Mineral, then go east to the castle. Tours are conducted Thursday through Sunday from 11:00 A.M. to 4:00 P.M. There's a fee but it's worth it. You don't find architecture like this anymore.

MARCHING PAST SEPTUAGENARISM
Sun City

The Sun City Poms are trying their best to dispel the notion that the major activities in retirement communities are golf, bridge, and visiting the doctor. The group is composed of up to forty women, all of them well over age fifty, some of them past age eighty. Despite their age the women maintain a rigorous schedule that includes twice-weekly rehearsals and more than fifty performances per year.

The Poms were organized in 1979 as a cheerleading squad for Sun City softball games. Dance instructors Corinne and Roy Leslie came up with the idea in an effort to boost attendance. Eventually the women split into two groups, one for dancing and one for marching. The ten members of the dance troupe perform mainly at private functions; the marchers, about thirty of them, strut their stuff in parades and as cheerleaders for local dignitaries. They have been featured subjects in national and international news stories and receive fan mail from as far away as Japan.

The average age, according to assistant-director Phoebe Saunders, is between seventy and seventy-one. "After that," she said, "they usually want to retire and do things retirees are expected to do." But not all of them follow that pattern. Vera Kraker, one of the original Poms, was still marching at age eighty-four. And even after she reached her seventy-ninth birthday, Rose Ann Russo was marching right alongside her daughter, Palma Mitzel, who was doing cartwheels at age fifty-nine.

The groups hire out for expenses and donations. For information, call (602) 392–4242.

FENCING WITH HISTORY
Tempe

Sue Faulkner's primary reason for putting a fence around her front yard was to keep her dog at home. But during the process the project also became a history lesson told in steel.

Faulkner is an artist who started her career by creating three-dimensional wire figures. She got into steel working after taking a welding class, so she bought a cutting torch. Her fence consists of figures cut from sheets of 14-gauge steel. It traces the history of Tempe from the time of the ancient Hohokam settlements of 600 years ago to the present.

Her original plan was to tell the story of Arizona. But she decided that subject was too broad, so she selected Tempe's history as her model. Prior to igniting her blowtorch, Faulkner spent months in local libraries and museums researching the city's past. Her *Portrait of Tempe* begins with sunrise on the

When she needed a fence to contain her dog, Tempe artist Sue Faulkner opted to make it also serve as a history lesson.

east side and concludes with sunset on the west. In between are her impressions of pioneers, railroads, schools, art, and architecture, all in chronological order and noted by dates welded onto the steel railings.

The fence stands about 2 feet tall and is painted dark green. History buffs and art critics will find it at 711 East Lodge, west of the intersection of Rural and Bell de Mar Roads in Tempe.

A DOUBLE HERO
Tempe

The ordinary man would not give up a multimillion-dollar career as a professional athlete to go crawl through the mud. But then Pat Tillman is not an ordinary man.

Tillman was a starting safety for the Arizona Cardinals of the National Football League, earning a very healthy salary for knocking people down. But prior to the 2002 season, he turned down a three-year contract with the Cardinals worth $3.6 million. Instead he joined the U.S. Army to become a Ranger, a job that pays $18,000 a year.

The media had a field day exploring the reasons for his decision, but Tillman wouldn't talk about it, refusing every request for an interview. But those who knew him said it wasn't an unusual move for Tillman. A year earlier he had rejected a five-year, $9-million offer to join the Super Bowl champion St. Louis Rams because he preferred playing for the perennially bad Cardinals. During his college days at Arizona State University, he often climbed a 200-foot tower to meditate. When he got bored he ran marathons, and he once competed in a 70.2-mile triathlon.

When the time came to leave the team, he simply told his coaches he wanted to join the Rangers and train with his younger brother, who enlisted at the same time.

The Rams went to the Super Bowl without him. The Cardinals didn't.

The Little Dam That Could
Tempe

Tempe's Town Lake is a man-made impoundment in the Salt River bed. It's 2 miles long, 800 to 1,200 feet wide, and 7 to 19 feet deep. By using a rather complicated formula, officials have determined the lake contains 977,000,000 gallons of Colorado River water that the city buys from the Central Arizona Project.

And the only thing holding all that water in place is a series of inner tubes. They're not the kind people buy at a bike-repair shop, however. These are great big inner tubes. Each is an inch-thick rubber-fabric bladder that measures 225 feet in length and weighs 40 tons. The sections are bolted to concrete slabs at both ends of the lake.

According to the signs along the lake, the rubber dams can withstand floodwaters and debris higher than anything ever recorded. If there is a major flood, the dams can be deflated and reinflated in forty-five minutes. Other signs along the lake take a lighter look at life. One says, NOBODY OWNS WATER. DRINK SOME AND TRY TO KEEP IT.

A Good Hare Day
Tempe

Invasion by giant rabbits isn't always a science-fiction scenario of horror. Sometimes it can be a good thing. There's an example of that in Centerpoint Plaza in downtown Tempe,

*Fortunately, the giant rabbits of Tempe don't live on a
diet of giant carrots.*

where three huge hares welcome everyone from tots to camera
toters.

The trio of oversized bunnies sits next to a shaded fountain,
one resting, one grooming, and one standing guard. They're
bronze replications of blacktail jackrabbits, done by Tempe
sculptor Mark Rossi, and they're so popular that constant pet-
ting has worn the patina off their noses and paws.

They weigh between 1,000 and 1,500 pounds and range in
height from 8 to 14 feet. They don't require feeding, which is a
good thing. There isn't enough land available in Tempe to plant
all the bronze carrots they'd need.

YOUR VERY OWN KACHINA
Tonto Hills

L ooking for that perfect gift, something nobody else has and probably never will get? A giant kachina could be the answer.

There's a 39-foot-tall replica of a Hopi kachina standing 7 miles north of downtown Carefree in the Tonto Hills subdivision. Billed as the world's largest kachina, it weighs 14.5 tons and took four months to construct. E. V. Graham, the developer, had it built as an inducement to get his wife to move onto the property, which at that time was way out in the country. It was designed by Philip Sanderson and engineered by Carl Ludlow, both of Phoenix.

The statue, located on Old Mine Road off the Carefree Highway, is composed of nine concrete sections. They were poured beforehand and then assembled and painted on the site. Hopiraised vegetables were cast into the base of the statue, accurately indicating the four points of the compass.

The really keen thing is that the current owners, Patrick and Tijuana Trotter, have it up for sale. It was appraised at $850,000, and that was the original asking price, but the Trotters say they'll take the best offer. The price doesn't include moving it to your own backyard, however.

For details on the current market price of 39-foot kachinas, call Judith Traynor at (800) 373–3355.

This 39-foot concrete kachina can be yours for a mere $850,000 obo.

INDEX

ABOUT THE AUTHOR

Sam Lowe has lived in Arizona since 1969, which puts him into the loosely regulated "near-native" category. He worked as a columnist for the *Phoenix Gazette* and *Arizona Republic* for more than twenty-five years and was named "Humor Columnist of the Year" by the National Society of Newspaper Columnists in 1988. After retiring in 1999 he became a freelance writer. He and his wife, Lyn, live in a two-bedroom house in Phoenix. There's nothing unusual about them or the house. Well, maybe the billboard-size circus poster plastered across one wall in the garage.

Author Sam Lowe and a freeway pot.